Jeff Zorabedian

UNA LAMARCHE is a writer and unaccredited *Melrose Place* historian who lives in Brooklyn with her husband, son, and hoard of vintage *Sassy* magazines. She is the author of two young adult novels, *Five Summers* and *Like No Other*, and remains a member in good standing of the Baby-sitters Club Fan Club. Lena Dunham once favorited one of her tweets.

UNABROW

Misadventures of a Late Bloomer

Una LaMarche

A PLUME BOOK

PLUME

Published by the Penguin Group
Penguin Group (USA) LLC
375 Hudson Street
New York, New York 10014

USA | Canada | UK | Ireland | Australia | New Zealand | India | South Africa | China
penguin.com
A Penguin Random House Company

First published by Plume, a member of Penguin Group (USA) LLC, 2015

 REGISTERED TRADEMARK—MARCA REGISTRADA

LIBRARY OF CONGRESS CATALOGING-IN-PUBLICATION DATA
LaMarche, Una.
  Unabrow : misadventures of a late bloomer / Una LaMarche.
    pages cm
  ISBN 978-0-14-218144-7
  1. LaMarche, Una. 2. LaMarche, Una—Childhood and youth. 3. Young women—United States—Biography. 4. Mothers—United States—Biography. 5. Coming of age—United States. 6. Popular culture—United States—Miscellanea. 7. Conduct of life. I. Title.
  CT275.L25285A3 2015
  306.874'3—dc23
              2014021212

Printed in the United States of America
10 9 8 7 6 5 4 3 2 1

Set in ITC Esprit Std Book
Designed by Eve Kirch

For Sam

(Someday, this will explain a lot.)

Your life story would not make a good book. Don't even try.

—Fran Lebowitz

CONTENTS
OR, A CHRONOLOGY OF ERRORS

ACKNOWLEDGMENTS

There are probably hundreds, if not thousands, of people who I need to thank for helping this book come to fruition, because based on my understanding of the ramifications of time travel (which itself is based on repeated viewings of *Back to the Future* and *Back to the Future Part II*), every single decision and human interaction of mine up to this point has gotten me where I am today, and if I were to go back and try to change even the most minuscule detail, like, say, to urge my seventeen-year-old, prom-bound self to reconsider her unintentional geisha makeup and the case of Zima she would later drink in a stranger's hammock, then I might come back to 2015 to find myself missing limbs, or working on a cruise ship. So thank you to everyone I have ever met, bumped into, or ducked into an alley to avoid.

A few, however, deserve special mention. In rough chronological order: Thank you to my parents, Ellen and Gara, for bringing me into the world, fostering my twin loves of writing and excessive TV watching, and continuing to support me even after it became clear that I would probably write a book about you later in life; to my beloved sister, Zoe, for putting up with my diva behavior on family road trips, keeping me sane(ish) for twenty-seven years and counting, and agreeing to take care of my facial hair should I ever find myself on life support; to my extended family (both blood and marriage) and my incredible friends, for their encouragement and enthusiasm; to my inimitable agent, Brettne Bloom, who changed my entire life with a single e-mail, and who worked tirelessly with me to get a proposal into shape; to my amazing editor and biggest cheerleader, Becky Cole, for making me feel witty and hilarious while simultaneously seeing all of my crutches and flaws with a gimlet eye and gently plucking them out like stray eyebrow hairs; and to the fantastically talented editorial and production team at Plume, for making this book everything I ever hoped it could be.

Finally, to Jeff and Sam, the loves of my life: without you, I am nothing. This book is for you. You may also share it with your future therapists in the interest of saving time. (You're welcome!)

INTRODUCTION

When we were three, my best friend Salvador and I used to play a game we called "look in butt." It was doctor, essentially, but as we had no interest in heartbeats or hearing tests, we chose to focus solely on the anus. One of us would bend over and the other one would conduct the examination. What we were looking for, I can't say—stray He-Man figures? lost crayons?—but we took our work seriously.

For years afterward I assumed that look in butt was consensual—the only thing that tempered the humiliation of its existence was Sal's complicity—but my father finally broke it to me that he'd overheard us playing it once, and that Sal, as he'd removed his underwear, had turned and said to me gently, "Una . . . this is *wrong*."

My small, naked friend's words have echoed in my head countless times since—when I attempted to fracture my own ankle in order to get out of track practice; as I was trying on my first boss's ten-year-old daughter's shorts while alone in their apartment; when I opened my college minifridge to reveal nothing but a bottle of gin and a carton of milk, and I thought to myself, *Well . . . why not?*—but they haven't made much of a dent in my track record of personal shame and flawed judgment. "Una . . . this is *wrong*," I'll think. But then I'll do it anyway because, sometimes, you can't tell what the right thing is until you do the wrong thing. And the silver lining about missteps is that they can set us on a better path. We examine them closely and try to come away with something, if not profound, then at least enlightening.

In August 2009, I was newly married and still on birth control but had the poor judgment to watch the movie *My Life* while drinking a bottle of vinho verde. For those unfamiliar with the plot, it's a 1993 Michael Keaton vehicle about a man with terminal cancer who makes instructional videos for his unborn son. The poster shows a baby's hand reaching out for a grown-up hand, and the tagline is "Don't watch this movie with someone who is made uncomfortable by hysterical weeping."

I decided that I should start keeping a list of lessons for my future children, not only in the case of my untimely and extremely heart-wrenching demise, but also just, you know, in case I got lazy or forgot. I had done a study on memory in college and learned that every time your brain accesses a long-term memory—say, that time you tried to somersault off the top bunk into the laundry basket—it gets altered slightly before it's filed away again, so that, little by little, stories change, and their morals get murkier. I wanted to get all my hard-earned wisdom down on paper before it faded into the abyss of my consciousness, replaced by plotlines on *Girls* and the words to early '90s rap songs. (That said, this book references both *Girls* and early '90s rap songs, because I know my strengths.)

Even though I wrote these essays, charts, and lists with my future grown-up children in my mind's eye, *please do not give this book to an actual child* unless he or she shows signs of premature jadedness and is able to use the word "fuck" at least three ways in a sentence. This book is for adults only—although that makes it sound like there's a lot of sex in here, which there's not.

I wrote this for my fellow women and mothers, but also for

dads, dudes, trans people, precocious teenagers, octogenarians who refer to themselves as "pistols," and anyone who can barely take care of themselves. Peace, love, and metaphorical brother-hood are all nice ideas, but I think what unites us as a species is that we all have cringe-inducing memories that we vow never to tell anyone and never to let anyone else repeat. Oops.

XO
Una

AUTHOR'S NOTE

This collection, contrary to the sage words of Fran Lebowitz, quoted previously, is largely a work of memoir, so obviously I have to write this disclaimer now that we live in the post–James Frey era in which every nonfiction writer lives in fear of being slowly shamed to death and/or drowned in his or her own sweat on live television. Just so we're clear: Everything happened as written to the best of my memory, which is to say, hampered somewhat by copious amounts of red wine and way too much exposure to pop culture in my formative years (I can give you the full name of every character on the original *Melrose Place* but do not know my blood type or my grandmother's birthday). I changed a few names here and there to protect people's privacy, and had to fill in some details using the similarly wine-addled brains of family and friends, but there's no straight-up *lying*. You'll notice, for example, that nowhere in this book do I mention having once thrown marbles out a window at Joe Cocker, because it was actually my friend Anna who did that, not me, despite what I have been telling people for the past fifteen years.

UNABROW

Unabrow

My sister, Zoe, and I have this agreement that if I ever fall into a coma, she will come to the hospital every few days to visit me. This is not so that she can brush my hair or read to me from the latest tabloids (although that would be nice; I'd hate to have a brain bleed undo all my hard-earned knowledge of Kardashian genealogy); no, my sister will have a very specific and important job. She will be there to pluck my eyebrows.

Zoe, who is a nursing-school student, told me that hospitals actually have junior staff members who are hired to do this kind of thing—trim people's nails, shave their beards, etc. But if she thinks she's getting off that easy then she is sorely mistaken.

"How often do I have to come?" she'll ask, glancing reluctantly at her iPhone calendar. "Once a week?"

"*No,*" I gasp. "Every three days for the eyebrows, and at least every week for the mustache."

"You never said anything about a mustache," she grumbles.

"Oh, and you'll need to pluck three hairs from my chin once per lunar cycle. Two are very stiff and black, but one is freakishly long and white. You might have to poke around for it; it likes to hide."

"Yay," Zoe says.

Once she asked me what I would do if I got marooned on an island like the castaways from *Lost,* all of whom seemed to have clandestine access to spa-grade laser hair-removal devices and blow-dry bars.

"I'd bring tweezers," I told her.

"But your bags went down with the plane," she said. "You don't have them."

"I strapped them to my leg with duct tape. Or I'd sharpen rocks and use them as razors. Or fashion a jaunty *niqab* out of palm leaves."

I am a girl with contingency plans.

I do realize that most people's coma and plane crash preparations don't involve brow shaping, but I happen to be a special case. My God-given eyebrows are so thick that they have become the stuff of legend, albeit among a relatively small circle of people who care about my forehead (a circle that now expands to include *you,* gentle reader, so welcome, namaste, please enjoy the complimentary boxed wine and Nair samples).

I also had a very impressive library.

I emerged from the womb on April 13, 1980, not only with a full head of black hair, but with a matching set of tiny but unmistakable caterpillars above my eyes. By the time I was six, the two had joined, forming a fuzzy bridge over my still buttony nose. Had I been born in the fifties, my mother might have burned them off with lye or sent me to Ms. Hannigan's Home for Hirsute Girls, but unfortunately my parents were progressive idealists committed to raising confident children, and so blindly loved me the way I was. In the mid-1980s, the fashion and beauty industries had not yet begun targeting innocent prepubescent children, so I skipped happily into the great wide world totally unashamed of my Brooke-Shields-on-Rogaine look.

Neither of my parents has ever, to my knowledge, had a unibrow. My dad's whole family is French and German, and they tend to be born blond, so they are absolved of blame. My mother's father's family, however, comes from Russia, a country known primarily for its vodka and excessive body hair.

"Real" Family Tree

Swarthy but innocent

I'm not even going to deal with these Aryan freaks

Mental illness, but no hirsutism!

One cig, two brows

A lot of hair, but in his defense it was the '70s

Plucking ninja

UNABROW

That doesn't seem to make sense, does it? I've always suspected my ancestors have conveniently excised some members from our family tree.

Suspected Family Tree*

Leonid Brezhnev   Female Sasquatch   Frida Kahlo   Martin Scorsese

Brooke Shields   Bert   Peter Gallagher   Anthony Davis

Lourdes Leon   Brobee

UNABROW

Unconfirmed by genetic testing.

The moment I first remember being aware of my special genetic quirk was in fifth grade when a substitute teacher took over my class because our normal teacher, Mrs. Walling, had to have her gallbladder removed. I don't remember what the substitute looked like, but I do remember that in the middle of a lesson he stopped and stared at me. He leaned forward, smacking his palms on his desk and breaking into a toothy grin, and said, without a trace of menace, "Young lady, you have beautiful eyebrows. Don't ever pluck them!"

The whole class burst out laughing, and I sat there blushing in confusion and trying to figure out if the laughter was at me or at him.

Until that point I had never been made fun of for my eyebrows.

I got teased way more about being a Goody Two-shoes (and for peeing in my woolen tights this one time during a spelling quiz in third grade, and not changing out of them because I thought no one would notice, and having my friends make up a song called "Una Has a Butt That Smells Like Pee"). I know they weren't all blind, so I can only assume they were just distracted by my braces and fetching wardrobe, which relied heavily on leggings, cowboy boots, and oversize tie-dyed T-shirts. Maybe, since I'd moved from Austin, Texas, in 1988, my Brooklyn classmates just thought Texas grew 'em bigger.

That substitute teacher was just the first of many strangers to comment on my appearance. I suppose I should feel lucky that he was so kind. I'm glad my first taste of ridicule didn't come from the man who did a double take on the street and jabbed at his friend to gawk, or the group of Asian teenagers on the subway who kept shouting "Freak!" and then bursting into laughter, or the pervy photographer who said he wanted to take my picture because I had such an "interesting face." I took to putting my hand up to my forehead in public places, as if I had a permanent itch right above my nose. It wasn't subtle, but it was acceptable camouflage.

The saddest thing about my unibrow is that it would have been so easy to fix. I mean, it's sort of ridiculous, given how much it came to stress me out. It's not like I had something that defied medical science, like an extra head from an absorbed twin, or even a surgical problem like a vestigial tail or third nipple. Literally the only thing standing between me and the end of my suffering was a six-dollar pair of tweezers (which, come to think of it, probably only cost three dollars in 1992—I could have used one week's allowance and still had two dollars left over to spend on decoupaging my vanity with Brian Austin Green centerfolds from *Tiger Beat*).

I don't know why I didn't do anything about it sooner, but after decades of obsession I've developed two theories.

Theory 1: I Was Confused as to Which Decade I Was Living In

There is actually a frightening amount of evidence to support this. Growing up, my parents only had a thirteen-inch black-and-white TV. The first cassette tape I ever bought was KC and the Sunshine Band's *Greatest Hits*. (In case you're wondering, this is *not* a cool answer to give when someone asks about your first adolescent musical experience.) In eighth grade, I took to wearing prairie skirts and love beads. A popular girl in my class once asked me, point-blank, "Why are you *wearing* that?" and I'm pretty sure I just shrugged and pointed to the swirly peace signs adorning my polymer clay bead choker.

Theory 2: My Mom Was Sort of a Hippie

There's even more evidence to support this: She went to art school in the mid-sixties. She was at the March on Washington. She worships Bob Dylan. She didn't (still doesn't) shave her armpits. She keeps pictures of herself from the seventies wearing metal head-dresses and fright wigs. She sent me to a Waldorf kindergarten, where I was forced to make dolls out of corn husks. She claims that no one should sleep in underwear because their genitals "need to breathe." Not exactly the poster girl for our country's self-flagellating adherence to cultural stereotypes of femininity, which I appreciate as an adult but could have done without back then. Also, since my dad had a beard and mustache at the time, there may well not have been a single razor in the house for the duration of my pubescence.

That said, it *was* my mom who eventually introduced me to twee-zers. It happened on a weeknight, in our living room. I was four-teen and had finally confessed—to my great shame—that I did not feel beautiful in my natural state, no matter how many times my parents loudly assured me that I was, and that they were not just saying that because they were blinded by familial love, or perhaps the glint from my glitter retainer. She sat quietly for a minute and studied me with sad eyes.

"Would you like me to shape them for you?" she offered. I nodded mutely and then perched on a stool while she went to re-trieve the necessary tools from her fireproof safe or wherever she had been hiding them. As she went to work, tears rolled down my face, as much from relief as from the stinging pain. When my mother was done, she held up a hand mirror, and what I saw took my breath away. I had a one-inch gap between the thick, wild, wiry mess on my forehead. I had eyebrows, plural. It hadn't felt that good to finally have two of something since my right boob had grown in.

Of course, what I hadn't considered was that the only thing worse than being made fun of in junior high was to make an abrupt physical change immediately visible to all your peers. The next day, everyone asked about my eyebrows. It was a straightfor-ward enough question: *Did you pluck your eyebrows?* But for some reason I refused to admit it. I said no, that I had simply been trim-ming my bangs and "missed." I tried to seem nonchalant, but it didn't help that I did not actually have bangs.

The naked strip between my eyes was world expanding, a fol-licular gateway drug. Shortly thereafter, my mother took me with her to a salon that did brow shaping, in the hopes that we could achieve something better than two thick rectangles. The aesthetician had no idea what she was in for; I could see shock and fear in her eyes as I approached from across the room. But she gamely took on the challenge, chipping away slowly until she had transformed my sloppy dashes into two commas, floating across my forehead like stocky little sperm. On the floor beneath my chair, it looked like I'd had a haircut.

I coasted on my new double brows for a month or two, but eventually I took matters into my own hands and got hooked on plucking. At first I just dabbled, kept them looking neat, experimented with shapes and varying degrees of thickness. But as I neared the end of high school, I rebelled, slowly deleting my eyebrows until they became almost invisible. I tried to be stealthy, but it was about as subtle as Chris Christie suddenly wasting away from anorexia. My mother noted this transformation with frightening dedication, and we started having the kinds of conversations you would normally see on a cautionary Afterschool Special, if they made them about really insignificant physical traits.

"Honey," she said hesitantly as she made dinner and I did homework at the kitchen table, "I'm worried."

"Mo-om," I said. "I'm fine. Don't start."

"You look *sick*." Her eyes brimmed with tears. "Like *Whoopi Goldberg*."

"Whoopi isn't sick."

"Doesn't she have cancer?"

"No!"

"But, sweetie, she has *no eyebrows*."

"Because she shaves them off, Mom. Which is her choice."

"Well, I think it's awful. You know, when I was your age—"

"*Moooooooom, stoooooooooop.*"

"—I had gorgeous, thick eyebrows like you. And then I overplucked and now . . ." Her breath caught in her throat and she set down the organic pepper she was chopping. "Honey, they *don't even grow anymore*. I have to use a pencil."

When I failed to respond, it only made her angry.

"You don't know what you're giving up!" she yelled. "You're only sixteen. You have your entire life ahead of you!"

"Shut up! You can't tell me how to conduct my own personal grooming!" [Cue angry teenage flounce out of room.]

My mother was never a stage mother—unless that stage was my forehead. She was counting on me to live her shattered dream, so I'm not surprised that she was sad to see the unibrow go.

"Una's eyebrows are too thin, don't you think?" she once asked my ninth-grade science teacher during a PTA conference. She seemed convinced that if she couldn't change my mind one-on-one, she could beat me through polling.

In tenth grade I humored her, dressing up as Bert from *Sesame Street* for Halloween. Even the yellow face paint, orange nose, and blood dribbling down my chin (Bert was also a zombie) didn't put her off; she thought I looked *gorgeous*.

⌒

Physically, my unibrow problems have been over since junior high (give or take a few plucking lapses due to illness), but now that I'm a mother I've shifted my eyebrow focus to the fate of my son and his potential future siblings. For someone who once put on a Greenpeace T-shirt and asked strangers to save the whales (albeit under duress—see page 193), I devote a truly astounding amount of time to thinking about hair removal for young children. I obsess over the best way to handle the inevitable genetic legacy that I will pass on to my kids. For instance, does creamy infant skin react poorly to depilatory creams? What's more emotionally scarring: school yard taunts, or electrolysis in the second grade? *Can* you actually shave off a child's unibrow under the pretense of trimming his bangs?

Of course I'm not *actually* going to forcibly wax a toddler. Any halfway serious plots I had got tossed when one of MTV's Teen

Moms plucked her sleeping three-year-old's unibrow in 2013, raising media pitchforks. *That's it,* I told myself sternly, *I cannot share the parenting philosophy of an eighteen-year-old who already has a chin implant and a sex tape.* How would I have turned out if my mother had been a press-hungry reality star instead of the kind of person who took naked outdoor showers on vacation, even when we had guests?

I want to be prepared for the talk about the Big U, so I did what any brain-atrophied, digitally dependent millennial would do: some half-assed research on the Internet. And here is what I discovered: having a unibrow is actually a condition called "synophrys." Isn't that cute? I even thought of calling this essay "Synophrabulous!" but I didn't think anyone would get it. Anyway, there's not much about synophrys on the World Wide Web—if you can believe it, no one has ever thought to write a cultural history of unibrows. Most of the entries say things like:

> The unibrow conventionally has negative associations in western [*sic*] culture, and is the reason why many people remove excess hair between the eyebrows*

Oh, really, Internet? *No shit, Sherlock.* Here's a slightly more surprising take:

> If you have a unibrow you probably have tons of testosterone and a large penis.†

Why, thank you, kind sir! No hot dog here, but quite frankly, if I have too much testosterone, that would explain a lot more than

---

*FactGrabber.com, "where curiosity meets accuracy."
†User "Wikko," mmo-champion.com/threads/1237262-Unibrow-Thread /page2.

my eyebrows. It would shed some light on why I chopped off my hair and insisted on playing with He-Man figures as a child, or why I was the only girl in my preschool class to cross heteronormative lines on Halloween by dressing as Peter Pan. Sadly, it would not explain the Donnie Wahlberg doll I purchased circa 1990, at the height of NKOTB mania. If I am really a man, I must be gay.

But let's assume for a minute that we're talking about a natural-born, estrogen-filled, penisless woman who just happens to have the facial hair of Early Man. Surely there must be some place on earth where this is *not* accepted as an automatic cause for mockery? Aha!

> In some non-Western cultures this facial hair does not have a stigma, and may even be seen as a sign of feminine beauty, as in Russia or in Iran, where connected eyebrows are a sign of virginity and a large dowry of goats.*

That's interesting. Jeff, my husband, is third-generation Armenian American, which places his ancestors right between Russia and Iran (a fact he had to inform me of, as I am worthless at geography). While I didn't have a unibrow when we met, maybe he could sense it there, like a phantom limb, and heard the voices of the elders whisper, *"This is the virgin for you."* Unfortunately, I suspect, the correlation between synophrys and celibacy is one of cause and effect. (He also got screwed on the goats.)

There's a book I found called *The Eyebrow* by Robyn Cosio, who, somewhat unsurprisingly, had a unibrow as a young woman. There is a reason that all the trainers on *The Biggest Loser* were invariably fat as children; emotional scars are best scrubbed clean

*Uncyclopedia.wikia.com, "the content-free encyclopedia."

by attempting to educate others about your affliction. Anyway, Ms. Cosio writes—without a footnote—that in ancient Greece:

> An eyebrow that marched in a single line, from one edge of the right eye, over the nose, to the edge of the left eye . . . was prized as a sign of intelligence and great beauty in women. If a woman was not blessed with one very large and very thick eyebrow, she was allowed to close the gap between her eyes with paint made of coal or lampblack. Or she simply put on false eyebrows.

Oh, Robyn. Ye of the selfsame name as my favorite Swedish pop star. Why must you taunt me with this imaginary utopia, in which I could have been the Angelina Jolie (or, okay, let's be realistic—the Marcia Gay Harden) of Sparta? I never had this knowledge growing up, and since most Americans with unibrows are villainous cartoon characters, my only positive role model was the Mexican artist Frida Kahlo. Kahlo famously exaggerated her unibrow and visible mustache in her paintings of herself, which some art buffs interpret as deliberately unflattering.

Purposefully unflattering or not, Kahlo remains the sole icon of female unibrow self-acceptance. One of her most famous paintings, her 1940 *Self-Portrait with Thorn Necklace, Hummingbird, and Unibrow*, acknowledges it outright. That is actually a really good idea; I might steal that from her. Instead of seeing my old photos as unflattering relics, I can turn them into art. My twelfth birthday party will heretofore be known as *Self-Portrait with Oversize Denim Hat, Slap Bracelet, and Unibrow*.

⁀

"I clipped an article for you from the *Times* magazine," my mother announced the other day. She handed me a folded piece of glossy paper with a look that seemed awfully smug for someone who still cut articles out of magazines with scissors instead of forwarding an e-mail link like a normal person. "Thick eyebrows," she said, "are back *in*."

I smiled and thanked her, tucking the clip into my pocket. I didn't have the heart to tell her that when people in fashion say "thick," they don't actually mean *thick*. These are the same people who hold up Anne Hathaway—whose breastbone can be seen from space—as an example of a "curvy" body type. So when they say that thick eyebrows are suddenly "in" again, they are basically joking. They are not inviting the women of the Caucasus to come and pose on the cover of *Vogue*, and I'm both relieved and surprisingly embittered by this. It's very confusing to define so much of your inner identity by an exterior trait you no longer possess. (Jennifer Grey, if you're reading, I know you feel me on this.)

I would like to be a more unself-conscious person and to let my freak flag fly right in the middle of my face. I also wish I could discover a stray chin hair without screaming, *"Don't look at me!"* to an empty house and then pratfalling into the bathroom with a pillow clutched over my face. I wish I could imagine a desert island scenario in which I was not frantically searching for sharp rocks with which to jab at my forehead, but rather enjoying the sun and, hopefully, having a tryst in a waterfall with Sawyer. But if wishes were horses, then beggars would ride—and I would have to get over my phobia of their enormous Chiclet teeth.

So I'll probably just continue to make endless self-deprecating jokes about my unibrow until I die or I slip into the coma that haunts my sister's nightmares. Because being loud about it is the only way that I know how to find other members of my tribe: yet-to-peak former outcasts with the dreaded "good personality" of the previously homely. I just don't feel safe otherwise. I mean, I can't trust anyone who never had an awkward phase in high school.

Those people are the *real* freaks.

THE SEVEN DEADLY SINS OF DIY BANGS

We've all been there.

It's a weekend afternoon. Your parents/roommate/spouse/children are out doing something productive and you are sweat-stuck to the couch, wearing a top or pants but definitely not both.

You think about taking a shower. You walk to the bathroom, because when it comes to personal grooming, showing up is half the battle. (The other half of the battle is remembering to shave both legs, and then return your parent's/roommate's/spouse's razor to its cradle without any visible hairs.)

But before you even make it to the shower, you see your reflection in the bathroom mirror (sin #1) and make a horrified face, à la Dr. Kimberly Shaw when she dramatically tore her wig off on season two of *Melrose Place*. Only you, sadly, have no wig to remove; you have not recently faked your own death, and that is your real hair.

What can I do to instantly improve my appearance? you ask yourself. You look around for tools. There's a toilet plunger, which would probably only make things worse. There's a toothbrush, which is no help because you've already uncorked the wine. Your eyes fall on a Walgreens brand mud mask that you purchased sometime in 2007, and even though it has hardened to an impenetrable solid, you reason that it might be difficult to knock yourself unconscious with it on the first try. And that is really your best choice because you look like Tom Hanks in *Cast Away* . . . *after* he lost Wilson. Yeah, it's bad.

It is only then, in an emotional state best described as "umbrella Britney," that you see the scissors. They're nail scissors, but hey, tomato, to-mah-to, right?

I don't know when bangs became such a facial game-changer. I think we can safely blame Zooey Deschanel, who seems to have had a falling-out with the real estate above her eyeballs circa the mid-aughts. (Worshipping false bang idols like Deschanel, Taylor Swift—and even, Bo forgive me, FLOTUS—is sin #2!) But we all secretly think we would look good with bangs. And so, without fail, you—the you who has neglected to take care of basic needs like bathing or wearing both tops *and* bottoms—become convinced that not only do you *need* bangs, but you are capable of cutting them yourself (sin #3).

You can totally do this, purrs the slovenly, pantsless devil on your shoulder. *Remember the last time you got your hair cut? It was so easy; you don't need to pay anyone. Just pull the hair straight up, snip, and loudly speculate as to whether Stacy Keibler was George Clooney's beard.* *

Ugh, she totally was, you think, as you pick up the scissors (sin #4). *She is a retired professional wrestler who was on* Dancing with the Stars, *for God's sake. She wasn't even a beard; she was a Billy Bob Thornton soul patch.*

You fold some of your hair over your forehead and mug for the mirror. You pretend you are Katy Perry at the VMAs and that you are wearing a bra made of gummy bears. *Yes,* you think, *I can totally rock bangs.*

Totes McGotes! cries the devil on your shoulder.

You hold the hair out in front of you, obscuring your vision. You snip (sin #5), visualizing a sexy, openmouthed Jennifer Garner (sin #6; no one looks sexy that way in real life).

You examine your handiwork and find that you have cut at a forty-five-degree angle from your left eyebrow to your right earlobe. You cut again. This time you've gone too short on the right side. *Maybe I should quit while I'm ahead and go to a salon,* you think, a cool breeze of sanity that blows right through your ears.

Then you remember that you still have to shower and shave and either wash or set fire to the sinkful of dishes before your

---

*I wrote this before you got engaged, George; please forgive me.

This is just one example of "sexy open mouth" gone wrong.

parents/roommate/spouse/children return. You soldier on (sin #7a), snipping away like a sculptor trying to reveal the masterpiece trapped in a block of marble.

And five minutes later, you step back and look in the mirror (sin #7b), to reveal your new, inch-long fringe.

It is your *David*, your *Mona Lisa*, your rheumy-eyed portrait of an elderly Kate Middleton. It is your eight-months-early Halloween costume as Lloyd—Jim Carrey—in *Dumb and Dumber*. And it is entirely your fault.

Remember, only you can prevent the devastating side effects of unprotected banging. Be smart. Stay safe.

What's Happening!! . . .
to My Body?

By the time I was six years old, I had given birth multiple times. It always started in a plastic hamper I referred to as my "dress-up closet," where I would select the perfect kimono for what I knew was sure to be both a physical and an emotional ordeal. I knew this because my mother, who taught childbirth education classes, had let me watch a VHS tape called *Birth in the Squatting Position*, which taught me that (a) babies usually came out looking like angry Smurfs and (b) giving birth involved a lot of wincing, moaning, and writhing around while holding what looked like a wet coconut between your legs. It was a young actress's dream role.

The kimonos (along with molting feather boas and floor-length nightgowns) were relics from my own mother's days as an urban bohemian, back when she traipsed across continents in platform boots and a rabbit fur coat, making abstract, labia-shaped sculptures and running into Rudolf Nureyev outside Studio 54. But after years of dress-up use, they were wrinkled and threadbare and bore the faint but unmistakable odor of cat piss. I didn't care. I accepted the pee smell as part of the journey to motherhood and simply imagined, as I tied on my birthing robe, that it was my signature sachet.

After stuffing my chosen spawn against my ribs, I would contort my tiny body in theatrical pain and hop up and down until my "baby" fell to the floor with a thud. My children were as diverse as they were synthetic. I gave birth to Cabbage Patch dolls, to sad-eyed Pound Puppies, and to fully dressed Peaches 'n Cream Barbies, who looked like sherbet-colored jellyfish crossed with Tammy Faye Bakker.

Ever the nurturer, I would "feed" my babies by pounding their heads against my concave chest or by smearing peanut butter across their faces like war paint. And after a few minutes, when I inevitably tired of parenthood, I would toss them in the pee basket with the cat and go have a snack.

You know, just your average six-year-old's birth story.

⌒

A woman's relationship with her body is based on such an advanced amalgam of math, physics, and behavioral psychology that I don't think anyone would pass it if it were a written test. It couldn't be standardized anyway, since everyone's equations are totally different. Even just to get the numbers you're working with, you'd have to calculate things like:

- (*cultural standards of beauty* [culture you're from] / *cultural standards of beauty* [culture you live in]) × (*waist-to-hip ratio* / $\sqrt{pie}$ [in pounds, consumed so far in lifetime]) = objective attractiveness

- *objective attractiveness* / (*number of awesome and loving relatives/mentors/lovers* − *number of manipulative and/or abusive/dickish relatives/mentors/lovers*) × *total lifetime exposure to Angelina Jolie's face* [in minutes] $^{number\ of\ Facebook\ profile\ photos\ you've\ taken\ of\ yourself}$ = subjective attractiveness

- *subjective attractiveness* × (*number of years of formal*

education / *number of seasons watched of* America's
Next Top Model) = gross confidence

- *subjective attractiveness* × *gross confidence* / $\infty^{number\ of\ current\ fashion/lifestyle\ magazine\ subscriptions}$ = net confidence

See? Gah. Already too much math, and we haven't even added in crucial factors like age, income, relationship status, the ability to pull off bangs, or that pair of pleather jeggings you may or may not have bought after a three-mimosa brunch.

Please understand that I'm not trying to make light of the serious, worldwide epidemic that is the commodification, sexualization, and simultaneous hatred of women's bodies. It's disgusting and depressing, whether you're talking about the politics of reproductive rights or the kind of hormone-laced-corn-fed culture that leads eight-year-olds to menstruate and kindergarten girls to dabble in anorexia. But these are the times we live in; body dysmorphia is the new black. I can write an entire chapter based on the breezy assumption that most women—if not most humans—hate their corporeal forms on some level, no matter where they fall on the body mass index spectrum. Amirite, laydees? Ugh, Jesus, let's just have a drink and get on with it.

Anyway, once upon a time, long ago and not at all far away since I still live six blocks from where I grew up, I can vaguely remember being nonjudgmental about my body. This was back in my birthing kimono, salad days, when I marveled at what my body could do—or at least *pretend* to do—as if I were the only person alive who had attempted such heroic feats as leaping from the coffee table onto a pile of couch cushions, sliding down an ice-covered stoop on my butt, or swinging so high and fast at the playground that the support beams shuddered.

I had a lot of insecurities as a kid. I was sort of unspecifically scared most of the time, even when—or, come to think of it, *especially* when—I was doing things that were supposed to be lifeaffirmingly, pants-shittingly fun for people in my age group. For example, since we lived in New York my parents would take me and a friend or two to the Big Apple Circus every year. Unlike the big, corporate Barnum & Bailey game, the Big Apple was a cozy affair with a single, European-style ring where clowns would often invite people from the audience to participate in things like throwing pies and helping a small dog to ride a unicycle. Sometimes performers would squirt water at us or try to sit in our laps. All of these possibilities terrified me to the point where I couldn't even pay attention to the acts because my brain was too busy calculating how I might quickly find an exit door or spontaneously self-immolate in the event that I was pulled onstage in front of thousands of peanut-chomping hecklers who might not see the delicate beauty my parents saw in my oversize Bart Simpson T-shirt, Technicolor stirrup pants, and jauntily crossed front teeth. So I was a panicky preteen, yes. But my fears were never rooted in my body.

That all changed when, at age twelve, my mother gave me the classic puberty manual *What's Happening to My Body?* I'm not saying this sensitive maternal gift was a curse or anything; however, *curiously* it was exactly around this age that my physical being began to betray me. From birth to age eleven, my body had been just that—a body. The thing that moved me from place to place and let me climb jungle gyms and eat french fries and make up totally unironic interpretive choreography to the *Dirty Dancing* soundtrack with my cousins. My skin fit perfectly and it never even occurred to me to look critically at the real estate below my neck. The only embarrassing thing that my body did, as far as I was concerned, was fart—and even that was kind of funny if correctly timed.

But then, the summer I was twelve, I grew breast. That's right: breast. Singular. I'll spare you the details, except to say that was also the summer I spent at a Quaker sleepaway camp with communal showers. And making matters worse, I was hairless but for my legs, which had somehow sprouted twin sea-otter-like pelts—seemingly overnight—and for my forehead, where I was cultivating a unibrow that would make Anthony Davis do a spit take (see page 4).

I had become suddenly, visibly, painfully pubescent, and the book helped reassure me that I was normal, which was a tough sell seeing as my only previous exposure to illustrated genitals was the R. Crumb anthology I'd paged through as a four-year-old in my bachelor babysitter's Upper West Side apartment, mistaking it for a children's book. (Incidentally, the same babysitter and I would later make up fantasy stories about Ronald and Nancy Reagan visiting a fantastical place called "Big Butt Island." I'm pretty sure my parents didn't pay him anything extra for these invaluable lessons.) Anyway, poring over those line drawings of puffy aureoles and patchily haired testicles, I turned a corner and came of age. My body morphed abruptly from a utilitarian vessel to an untrustworthy stranger.

THE SEVEN STAGES OF CORPOREAL METAMORPHOSIS FOR HUMAN BEINGS—OR MAYBE JUST WOMEN? I DON'T KNOW, BUT THIS IS STILL VERY SCIENTIFIC, I PROMISE

I. Body as Magic

Although I have come close to replicating it with certain pharmaceutical substances, I don't remember this stage firsthand. So it's lucky that I've been able to study and rediscover the mind-blowing period of early physical consciousness through my son. This encompasses the first two years of life, give or take, when every single thing the body does is trippy, primal, and existential in the purest meaning of the word. An abbreviated chronology of this stage can be summarized by the following inner monologue:

> *What?! CHECK ME OUT! I am here. I can see things! I can hear things! I can make sounds! Whoa, I have toes! I think I can fit them in my mouth! Ahhhhh, fingers! Must touch everything. Must. Grab. EVERYTHING. What else can fit in my mouth? Sitting! Sitting upright!!! Who is that in the mirror? Who is that marvelous creature? Will he mind if I give him a sloppy kiss? No, he doesn't! He's KISSING ME BACK! OMG, OMG, I'm crawling!!!!!! Now I'm standing!!!!!!! WALKING, SUCKAS!!!!!!!!!!!!!! NOW I'M RUNNNINGGGGGG-GGG!!!!!!!!!!!!! CLIIIIIIIIIIIIIIIIIIMBING!!!!!!!!! Nothing can stop me now! Look out, world . . . and small house pets!*

II. Body as Vessel

This is the aforementioned period of unwitting bliss during childhood (typically age three to about ten or eleven, if you get lucky and don't have any physical disabilities and/or body-shaming adults in your life) when the body is completely disregarded, assuming it can perform all its basic functions without incident. Sure, you might want to be able to jump higher or hit a baseball farther or learn to cartwheel, but you never look at your legs and think, *God, my thighs are like Easter hams! I* have *to start doing Pilates!* Instead, you look at them and think, *Legs.* Because that is all they are. And then you use them for their intended purpose, which is to kick your brother.

III. Body as Stranger

Perhaps, like me, you grew a single breast or had the kind of unfortunate hair growth pattern that prompted the most popular girl in your seventh grade class to ask, "Do you shave just the *backs* of your legs?" during lifeguard training. Or maybe one day in social studies, you found yourself searching the room for the source of a pungent, sour milk smell only to realize with horror that the call was coming from inside the house—or, more specifically, from inside your shirt—and that deodorant was about to become a priority in your life, second only to examining your pubic mound every night for new hairs. Whatever it is, these first awkward whiffs of puberty (usually around age eleven or twelve) catapult your physical being into a strange new universe of significance. The body, once a steadfast, invisible ally, is now a dangerously loose cannon gunning for the spotlight. Cystic acne, fat deposits, an ill-timed erection—any of these could befall you at any time. You would sleep with one eye open if you weren't so exhausted from the twice-daily full-body washes you must endure to control your new hormonal stench.

INTERMISSION:
A REAL DIARY ENTRY THAT I WISH WERE FAKE

> *August 16, 1994*
> *GUESS WHAT?! I got a tampon in. I thought I was de-*
> *fective and had two orifices or something but NO! YAY! I*
> *am so proud and relieved. Let us mark this day in history!*
> *Much love, Una*

I am not kidding when I say that this was by far the most exciting entry my diary had ever seen up to that point. Had I started
to write my autobiography in 1994, the Great Tampon Victory
would surely have been the highlight, deserving three or four
chapters. The rest of this volume, which spans the summers of
1993 to 1997, recounts my days in the way that your ninety-year-
old great-aunt might: *Let's see, I had breakfast—grapefruit—and
then I watched that Geraldo on TV. I read for a while and went to the
pharmacy for my Coumadin. We had hamburgers for supper.* I pep-
pered my writing with declarations of love for unrequited crushes,
but I never had so much as a study date to write to my diary about.
I can only imagine that my all-caps GUESS WHAT?! elicited my
jaded diary to respond, *What, did we fall asleep reading John
Grisham and dream about Evan Dando again?*

In my defense, I later had a boyfriend who began his diary
entries with the words "Dear Jesus," so it could be worse.

IV. Body as Object

This stage, I think, is felt most acutely by women. Once you make
it through the craters of puberty (this age differs for everyone, but
a good rule of thumb is to find the page in your parents' photo albums in which the photos resume normally after a series of years
in which they have been crudely defaced with marker or ripped

out in order to be ritually burned) you will be understandably in-secure. Your body has up and *Scooby-Doo*'d you, pulling off its kindly mask to reveal a villainous wretch. And it is just when you are getting used to the new you—the taller, curvier, muskier you with boobs and hips and more places to shave—that adults begin to notice you in new and unwelcome ways. This is the phase during which catcalls will come into your life, but since you are still technically a girl, not yet a woman, to paraphrase Britney Spears, they will mystify you at first. Eventually, they will come to humiliate you, and make you want to retreat into the safe, smooth, flat planes of your child body, which brings me to the next stage.

V. Body as Nemesis

It's Very Special Episode time; bear with me. This one is going to be longer and more poignant. It's like the Sweeps Week of this list. I even have celebrity cameos!

I'm going to speak for myself, and not pretend I'm representing all of womankind, mostly because I still harbor a deep-seated but dubious hope that I represent the exception and not the rule. For me, coming out of puberty (or, really, out of teenagehood, because I was and continue to be a late bloomer) dovetailed with starting to view my body as my enemy, which spiraled into an eight-year battle with anorexia and bulimia.

I know. Not two hundred words ago I was writing about *Scooby-Doo* and Britney Spears and now we've taken a detour into my most painful secrets. It's weird for me, too, and I'm really uncom-fortable letting that just sit there without a self-deprecating joke to soften it. But there's nothing funny about eating disorders, and I'm not going to pretend that there is. Remember that FX comedy series *Starved*, about an eating disorder support group? Right, neither does anyone else. (And this is FX! The channel that built an *entire episode* of *It's Always Sunny in Philadelphia* around seeing Danny

DeVito take a dump on the floor of a bar! If there were anything uproarious about bulimia, surely FX would have discovered it.)

So, this unhappy stage—which doesn't affect everyone and which definitely does not automatically include eating problems— can last a long time. Chances are, once you get accustomed to your flamboyant new adult body, you begin to target perceived flaws. You might look at yourself and think, *How can I be prettier? How can I be more desirable to the people of whatever gender I lust after? How can I get noticed?* Or you might have the opposite reaction: *How can I become invisible again? How can I get back into a body that doesn't betray me or attract unwanted attention on a daily basis?* Unfortunately, the answer to all of these questions is usually the same: lose weight. Because that is the enormous mind-fuck that our culture has succeeded in selling across all racial, political, and socio- economic lines: that the taut flatness of prepubescence represents the height of both sexual desirability and asexual innocence.

I wish I knew how to skip over the Body as Nemesis stage. For me, it took a lot of therapy, practice, and false starts, as well as the acceptance that I should never, ever buy another pair of capri pants, not even on sale, if I ever want to really love myself the way I truly am. But one hard-and-fast rule I have walked away with is this: *don't read lists of other people's daily calorie intakes.*

You'd think this would be an easy enough thing to avoid, but if you look around, they are everywhere. Magazines just love to ask celebrities what they eat in a day. Unless the celebrity in question is a hot-dog-eating champion, there is no way to pretend this is news, so instead they try to pass it off as either (a) an aspirational primer for those mere mortals who can't afford to stock fresh wild salmon and/or make their own cashew butter or (b) a refreshing peek at a "totally normal" glutton who is "just like us" except also impossibly toned and mind-bendingly gorgeous despite his or her deep-dish stuffed-crust Domino's habit. *Do not buy into these lies.* There's no way the person is telling us everything. I mean, look,

Gwyneth Paltrow has built a brand for herself as a cheerful, macrobiotic foodie based on the implicit assumption that she has never found a Skittle under the stove, wiped it off on her pants, and then eaten it. But everyone has at some point in their lives done *this exact thing*, so *do the math, Gwyneth*.

P.S. In my early twenties—during the height of my illness—I used to fantasize that if I were ever granted powers of invisibility (this was right around the first *Lord of the Rings* movie), I would use it to follow around skinny celebrities and find out what they *really* ate all day. Yes, you read that right; I decided to use my hypothetical superhuman powers not for good, or even for middle-school revenge-based evil, but for the kind of research task that might be delegated to a summer intern at *Shape* magazine.

VI. Body as Magic, Part 2

By the time you've lived in your body for thirty years or so, there's not much it can do to surprise you anymore. All its sounds and smells and unsightly bulges have been cataloged and then either frantically hidden or hopelessly ignored. Which makes it all the more shocking when your body up and does something you never thought possible. Which, in my case, was to make a cuter, littler body inside of mine. In 2011, I became a human version of Hasbro's Puppy Surprise doll, a bucket list goal I had been gestating since the mid-1980s.

Not everyone's magic is childbirth. Obviously I'm excluding half of the population outright,* and plenty of women decide either not to have children or to have them via adoption or surrogacy. But I've heard similar stories from marathon runners, disease survivors, and, memorably, a backup dancer from Madon-

---

*And do not talk to me about the "pregnant man." He had a uterus. I will be amazed when a man carries a baby in his scrotum, okay?

na's Sticky & Sweet tour (of whom I am insanely jealous). Something incredible happens when you endure a grueling physical challenge, either by choice or by fate. It changes your body, and your relationship to your body, forever.

Since I am lucky enough never to have suffered a major illness or been forced to run more than fifty feet in my adult life, I'm here to talk about the transformative experience of baby making. There's nothing else remotely like it, and even making up an analogy ends up sounding ridiculous. Like, imagine for a moment that puppies grew in fanny packs. If you wanted a dog, you'd get this bulky, retro, flesh-colored albatross to hang around your waist (let's say it costs a thousand dollars, which is probably the minimum you'd spend on prenatal care even with insurance) and then you'd lug it around with you at all times for nine months while it got heavier and heavier. People would constantly exclaim over the fanny pack and rub it affectionately, and then they'd give you an ice-cream sundae and instruct you to go to town. But one day, the fanny pack would burst open and a needy puppy would leap out and immediately shit on you, and then you'd have to chase it around until you died. I kind of don't think anyone would get a dog under those circumstances, do you?

That said, pregnancy was a thrill for me. I had fetishized the pregnant bellies that streamed through my living room throughout childhood, and to finally be the owner of one was a dream come true. It helped that I didn't suffer from much nausea and already owned an impressive collection of elastic-waist pants. I would strip down to my skivvies every day, look in the mirror, and caress my tumescent belly like I was starring in an Internet fetish video. And rather than worry about the weight I was gaining, I focused my perfectionistic efforts on making sure I was gaining enough. For nine months, there was nothing I ate that couldn't be improved by a topping of cheese, avocado, or ice cream. It was catharsis à la mode.

But all good things must come to an end, and the gift of pregnancy ended with a decidedly less bucolic sensation. Some of you know what I'm talking about and are reflexively Kegeling from the sense memory. For the rest of you, I would like to attempt to describe what natural childbirth feels like.

No one has actually asked me what it felt like to push a baby out of my body without drugs, but I feel it's a public service, because when *I* Googled "What does childbirth feel like?" in order to try to do a *Karate Kid* montage of intense mental and physical preparation, all I found was a bunch of Yahoo! message board posts in which women basically just said that it hurts.

Before I gave birth, I kept joking to my horrified mother that I was going to live-blog the experience, but even if I'd done that it wouldn't have clarified anything for you. It probably would have looked something like:

5:50 a.m.: *First contraction!!!!*
5:55 a.m.: Shit, these are close together.
7:30 a.m.: Owwwwwwwww.
8:00 a.m.: [*Retching sounds*]
8:30 a.m.: FUCK EVERYONE IN THE FACE.

In between contractions, I focused on looking pretty.

10:00 a.m.: Hi, guys, this is Jeff. Una says if I try to get her to type anything else into her phone she's going to kill my entire family. She's mostly screaming now. It sounds like Gilbert Gottfried got stuck in a garbage disposal.

1:00 p.m.: Jeff again. I can never unsee this.

1:30 p.m.: I've been to hell and back. Baby is bare-assed; I'm wearing a diaper. How is this fair?

So before I block it out completely I'd like to document my birth as best I can. Obviously, everyone's experience will be different. One woman's stabbing vagina pain of death is another woman's unrelenting, shooting genital hellfire.

First things first, I skipped early labor. That's the beginning stage in which you supposedly feel relatively mild contractions every half hour or so, but can still do things like bake cookies, watch movies, and walk places without crying. So I don't know what that feels like, but compared to active labor I'm going to assume it feels like dry-humping the Stay-Puft Marshmallow Man.

Active labor, for me, felt more or less as follows: First, it's like the baby is putting a corset on you, but making it too tight on purpose so you'll pass out at the cotillion and ruin your chances of ever dating the heir to an oil fortune. The pain of contractions wraps around your belly and shoots down through your pelvis. At first you can breathe through them, but soon you have to moan and then yell into a pillow. The corset is suddenly made of knives, and they are stabbing you where the sun don't shine.*

The worst part was "transition." Unfortunately this does not mean a soft dissolve into the next scene, in which you are holding your beautiful newborn and simultaneously eating a whole pound cake. No, in this context the word "transition" means that you are

---

*I realize that's not very specific, since the forty-week pregnant belly casts a significant shadow. So, for clarity, what I mean is, in the genitals.

fully dilated and the baby's head is moving through your cervix. Of course, at the time I didn't know I was in "transition." I thought I was in Dante's heretofore-undocumented tenth circle of hell, except instead of Carrot Top attempting to give me an erotic massage, I was simultaneously splitting in half and feeling like I was about to shit on my duvet.*

I have outlined my other nine circles of hell below, for reference.

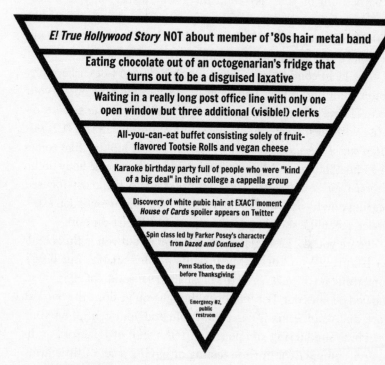

E! True Hollywood Story NOT about member of '80s hair metal band

Eating chocolate out of an octogenarian's fridge that turns out to be a disguised laxative

Waiting in a really long post office line with only one open window but three additional (visible!) clerks

All-you-can-eat buffet consisting solely of fruit-flavored Tootsie Rolls and vegan cheese

Karaoke birthday party full of people who were "kind of a big deal" in their college a cappella group

Discovery of white pubic hair at EXACT moment House of Cards spoiler appears on Twitter

Spin class led by Parker Posey's character from Dazed and Confused

Penn Station, the day before Thanksgiving

Emergency #2, public restroom

After transition comes pushing, which most people assume is the really painful part, but for me it was a bit of a relief, because I

---

*I gave birth in my house. On purpose. It was a little awkward telling the neighbors beforehand (it helped that I gave them wine and earplugs) but otherwise great.

got to be an active participant in the birth and not just a moaning, writhing, passive victim. From movies and TV you think that after pushing for five minutes the baby comes out, which is sometimes true for second or third births, but for first-timers pushing can last a few hours. But! The good news is that you won't know how long it's taking because you're too busy concentrating on each contraction—which now feels like you're attempting to push a barbell out of your ass—and the sweet, sweet sixty to ninety seconds of peace and painlessness you get in between them. The bad news, of course, is that it ends with a human head coming out of a place you equate with pleasure.

The head coming out hurts, I won't lie. I can't describe it any better than that it feels like what it is: a head coming out of your body. There's a stretching, burning sensation that gets more intense with each push. But by that point you're screaming, *"Get this thing out of me, noooooooooowwwwwww!!!!"* and looking like someone Photoshopped Nick Nolte's mug shot face onto the body of the *Exorcist* girl, so the pain takes a backseat to the most focused bearing-down you will ever do. Birth makes your worst poop experience seem like shooting feathers out of a T-shirt cannon.

There you go. Essentially, what I've just told you is that childbirth hurts. Who knew? My insights are invaluable. But here's something no one else says: the most alien sensation of all is when the body comes out. Because even though you've done the hardest part, and your cervix is passed out cold and your central nervous system is shuddering and pouring itself a shot of Jameson, nothing will prepare you for the feeling of having a set of little arms and legs pulled out of your abdomen and through your baby chute. It's not so much painful as it is incredibly weird. But then you get your wrinkled little spawn plopped on your chest, and the oxytocin starts flowing, and suddenly you *are* dry-humping Mr. Stay-Puft . . . with your heart.

And I never criticized my body ever again.

Hahahahaha. Lies. Of course I do. But it has gotten a lot better, with the exception of my vagina, which I choose no longer to look at, since the last time I did, it resembled an appliance that you try to shove back in its original box, but it won't fit, and there are cords and polystyrene peanuts hanging out. It was depressing, so we just e-mail now.

VII. Body as Frenemy

Once you have passed your peak of attractiveness and settled into a slow, steady, relaxing downhill slide, the body becomes no longer a bombshell or magician or villain, but something more along the lines of a wisecracking sidekick who mostly hangs back only to deliver a barb when you least expect it.

For example, one day not long after I gave birth, I looked down and noticed that my ass was gone. It had just cut and run—didn't say good-bye, didn't even leave a note. (Evidence suggested that my breasts had started to give chase but tired by the time they reached my lower ribs.)

"BUTT DISAPPEARED!" I frantically typed into my Google search bar, which has recently suffered through such wide-ranging queries as "celebrity photobombs" and "Outside of cheese wheel edible?" Alas, the Internet offered me no solace, only a variety of links to weight-loss message boards. And yes, I had lost weight: thirty pounds of baby weight plus seven extra pounds of constant breast-feeding, acute postpartum anxiety, and a diet that consisted almost exclusively of infant tears and orange Fanta. But still, it seemed unfair. I still had a belly as soft and pliable as fresh pizza dough, which merrily jiggled when my kid climbed into my lap for story time. Why couldn't *that* have magically melted away? Why should my butt be the one to pay for what my uterus had wrought? And where did it go? Did it follow the Reagans to Big Butt Island in the hopes of returning with a trunkful of junk? Did it become

invisible and travel to Los Angeles to stalk Lara Flynn Boyle? It
could have at least left a note.

⌣

As I encounter the first signs of real aging, I've started to wonder
why the *What's Happening* franchise—the book series, I mean,
not the '70s television show about urban black life in Los Angeles
(although I most definitely *would* watch *What's Happening!! ... to
My Body?*, especially if Rerun danced)—deals only with puberty.
Because while adolescence may be the first time our bodies play
tricks on us, it's certainly not the last. What of the postpartum
period? Perimenopause? Hospice? Herewith, a summary of my
findings thus far, both from personal experience and extremely
unscientific observation, otherwise known as "A Short(ish) List
of Physical Betrayals."

HAIR

No matter where you fall on the color spectrum, from Nick Cave
to Nicki Minaj, chances are that by your midforties you will find
enough shades of gray to create, if not a bestselling trilogy of erotic
novels, then at least a gross scrapbook. (Note: they're not all on
your head, these gray hairs. Get excited!)

FACE

Imagine a flipbook of John McCain's cheeks as he shoots through
a wind tunnel. Beginning at age thirty-five, each page represents
one year of your life.

EYES

During your twenties, you can call them "bright." If you can manage to say anything bitchy or insightful on a semiregular basis,

your thirties and forties can coast on the sassy adjective "gimlet," no matter the depth of your crow's-feet. After that, it may be best just to keep them closed.

NOSE

Never stops growing, regardless of truthfulness. Some individuals attempt to camouflage this ever-enlarging protuberance with a garden of colorful gin blossoms, which are permanent and aggressive perennials.

DÉCOLLETAGE

Derived from the French word *décolleter*, meaning "to be forced to wear crewneck sweaters due to the fact that the sun spots on your chest have joined to form one giant leather patch, sort of like the trash heap floating in the Pacific Ocean that can be seen from space."

HANDS

Evolution has taught us that primates are our closest mammalian relatives. But considering the slow transformation of once-youthful fingers into brittle, gnarled claws, I say: remember the bird.

BREASTS/PECTORALS

As you age, most parts of the body look better lying down, because the excess skin recedes into the blankets, revealing your original shape. Not so with the chest. It is only at this point in life that the true purpose of armpits is fully revealed: supine breast rests.

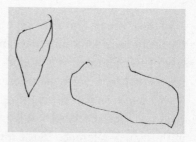

Drawing of my "bobos" by my two-year-old son, 2013.

ABDOMEN

The media encourages us to strive for "six-pack" abs, and while
that dream is deferred for most of us as we pursue loftier goals like
incubating humans or finishing a plate of mile-high nachos, it can
be helpful to think of the torso as a six-pack of beer. With each
decade, beginning at birth, take away one can, until they are all
gone and you are left with a warped, stretched-out set of rings.

ELBOWS/KNEES

Begin winking. This is less delightfully coy than one might hope.

THE DREADED Q WORD (LADIES ONLY)

Ugh, I cannot say—or even type—this word. It makes me cringe
with humiliation. But you all know it. It starts out like the band
fronted by Freddie Mercury and ends like Joaquin Phoenix's original hippie name, which also happens to mean the thin, flat, often
green-colored organs of vascular plants such as trees. It also
rhymes with the last word of John Grisham's bestselling legal
thriller *The Pelican Brief*. It happens sometimes when your vagina
simply has too much to say and gets flustered, or when you attempt an inverted yoga pose. It is, quite simply, the worst.

⌒

And those are just my *external* findings. I haven't even mentioned
the decrease in serotonin that can lead to the unironic purchase of
cross-stitch patterns or Isotoner clogs, or the inexplicable popping
noises that sound off whenever you squat.

No one tells you these things. Nora Ephron tried to, but her
report was too specialized. What we need is a textbook, something
with a quick-reference index for things like "wattle" and "thut-
tocks" (the unfortunate result of a vanishing border between up-

per thigh and lower cheek, a term coined by noted anatomist Alyssa Milano). Because as it stands—or falls, since that's much more likely to be the case—it's a shock to the system. If you're anything like me, one minute you're trying to pick out the right size Super Ball to even out your training bra, and the next you wake up to find that some part of you has gone inexplicably missing—and you just can't find it anywhere.

Not even in the squatting position.

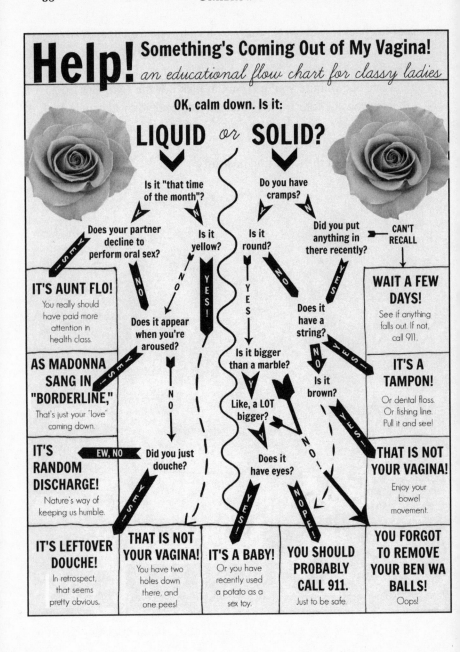

A Scar Is Born

Picture this: You are standing on an auditorium stage, cloaked in darkness. The audience, made up of your family, friends, entire elementary school class, and the original cast of *Beverly Hills, 90210*, titters nervously. They don't know what to expect. But you do. You have been waiting for this moment your entire life.

The spotlight comes on as the first note rings out across the cavernous room, and even though you're temporarily blinded you can tell from the audible gasps that you look amazing in your skintight, iridescent jumpsuit and high-heeled boots, your normally limp hair a halo of Diana Ross curls. You raise the microphone to your Dr-Pepper-flavor-Bonne-Bell-slicked lips and, feeling your heart thump in your chest like a drum circle of angels, sing the first lines of Madonna's "Like a Prayer."

Life is a mystery / Everyone must stand alone . . .

To everyone's shock and awe, you sound *exactly* like Madonna, and the fifth-grade orchestra sounds *exactly* like professional studio musicians—somehow they have even gotten their hands on an electric guitar and full-size church organ. Jason Priestley is al-

ready on his feet giving you a standing ovation before you've finished the first verse. And you allow yourself to smile a little bit,
knowing that the best is yet to come.

It was hard to find a gospel choir who would perform for your
pittance of an allowance. But as luck would have it, the very first
Harlem church you walked into in your immaculately white Reebok high-tops welcomed you with open arms, and when they
heard your sultry alto, surprisingly rich and sexual for someone
so young, tears streamed down the singers' faces as they closed
their eyes and swayed, waving their arms as if inviting God himself to bear witness to your gift. You made their robes at home,
dousing your mother's eggplant-colored bedsheets in glitter, and
when the moment arrives, as stagehands pull back the thick curtains to reveal two dozen sparkling backup dancers belting out the
chorus, a roar emanates from the crowd almost loud enough to
drown out the bass synthesizer. By the time the smoke machine
starts, and you are lifted into the air on your hidden platform to
bring it on home, news crews are bursting through the auditorium
doors, stumbling over each other in their haste to capture even a
moment of this miracle, to share with people who are suffering
and in need of a reminder that there is still magic in this world.

Are you still picturing it? Great. Now you know what it felt
like to live inside my head at age twelve.

Madonna's *Immaculate Collection* (1990) notwithstanding, almost all of my favorite music was produced between 1991 and
1994. Salt-N-Pepa, En Vogue, TLC, Boyz II Men, Kris Kross, P.M.
Dawn, Naughty by Nature, Arrested Development—these are my
totally unironic, nonguilty pleasures. Even one-hit wonders from
forgotten stars like Sophie B. Hawkins and the unfortunately sur-
named Ce Ce Peniston make me swoon. We would not be friends
if your instinct is to change the station when "To Be with You" by
Mr. Big comes on the radio.

And my obsession with the early nineties doesn't start and

The physical reality of age twelve was only slightly *less glamorous.*

stop with the Billboard Hot 100. I love saying "Boutros Boutros-Ghali." I own both a Cross Colours jacket and a stack of *Sassy* magazines that I won on eBay. No movie will ever be as perfect as *Reality Bites*. It is one of the great tragedies of my life that no men have ever battled for my heart by doing a sing-off of "Two Princes" by the Spin Doctors. I consider the Oscars a miserable failure if Billy Crystal doesn't enter on horseback, and despite how wrong it is, I still think Erik Menendez was hot. A part of me will always live in 1993.

Apparently there is science to back up this phenomenon of acute nostalgia. During adolescence we experience the fastest period of brain growth since the trippy crash course of infancy, so what we observe and learn between twelve and fourteen can stick in a way that's more indelible than what comes before or after. And hey, if I can blame my multiple Color Me Badd CDs on science, I'm gonna.

However, the small section of my temporal lobe not reserved for Sir Mix-a-Lot lyrics is engraved with more troubling recollections of the exquisite, crushing pain of early puberty. There are the physical betrayals, of course—here lie the seedlings of my lifelong unibrow obsession and my bloodhoundlike knack for detecting untreated body odor—but the emotional scars run even deeper, drawing a sense memory map across my nervous system that will forever link feelings of shame and sadness to pop culture escapism.

Let's start with insomnia and Garrison Keillor.

Obviously.

Every Saturday when I was young, my parents would listen to *A Prairie Home Companion* on the radio, and so it happened that at a very young age I fell in love with the slow drip of Midwestern molasses that was Garrison Keillor's voice. Since it was radio, I didn't know what he looked like, so I imagined my preadolescent crush, Sam Malone from *Cheers*. I would lie awake at night listening to tapes of *News from Lake Wobegon*, letting Keillor's languid, dusky baritone lull me to sleep.

My love for him was more personal than you might imagine the relationship between an awkward, anonymous East Coast preteen and a reasonably well-known middle-aged Midwestern radio personality might be. Because on my tenth birthday, my big gift was to see *A Prairie Home Companion* recorded live at the Brooklyn Academy of Music. On that memorable night, not only did I meet Keillor in the flesh, but he even said my name on the radio, in a surprise message from my parents. (He pronounced it "Ewena," which broke my heart a little, along with the fact that he looked more like an enormous human version of one of my troll dolls than Ted Danson, but my passionate yet nonsexual crush could not be extinguished.) I felt we were simply . . . simpatico. Just as Garrison had a story about his "storm home," in which he fantasized about running away into the arms of the childless strangers who'd been assigned him in the event that snow prevented the school buses from getting kids back to their rural houses, I imagined that if things ever got bad with my family—if they stopped letting me eat an entire pound cake for breakfast, say—I could stow away to Saint Paul, Minnesota, and knock on his door and he'd swing it open with a wry smile and a tip of his signature round glasses, sighing, "Well, if it isn't my little Ewe-na. I'd know you anywhere. Come in, child, have some cocoa, and let me play you a tune on the singing saw."

But until that day arrived, I was satisfied with listening to his voice every night on my cassette player. It became especially helpful when I started at a new school in seventh grade and needed extra comfort to offset my snowballing anxiety. Gary was there as I slipped between my sheets, there as I snuggled my Pound Puppy, Harold, and turned off the light. His voice massaged my soul as I snapped my sparkly retainer in place and then drifted off into hormonal dreams, which would find me finally making out with the more age-appropriate object of my affections, only to pause in order to take my retainer out halfway through. "Sorry," I would purr in the dream, in as lusty a voice as I could manage with a mouth so full of spit, "my orthodontist says I have to wear it all the time." The only saving grace of these dreams was that at least neither Gary nor Harold ever made an appearance.

One fateful night, however, my prairie home companion abandoned me. Just as I was losing consciousness, the tape deck snapped off abruptly, midway through one of Garrison's Lake Wobegon tales, leaving an eerie quiet punctuated every second by what I had never before noticed was the extremely creepy ticking sound of my Kit-Cat clock's plastic tail. That night I couldn't go back to sleep, no matter how hard I tried. Eventually I surrendered to wakefulness and spent the wee hours of the morning reading old Sweet Valley High novels with my knees tucked tight against my chest inside my flannel nightgown, hoping against hope that somehow my hatred of that entitled bitch Jessica Wakefield might cause me to spontaneously pass out, like a rage stroke.

I didn't know it then, but what I was feeling was my first grown-up fears slipping through the first cracks in my formerly impenetrable childhood self-esteem. Here I was in a strange new school, in a strange new body, feeling lost in a way that couldn't be fixed by finding the nearest adult and asking him or her to call my mom over the PA system.

I didn't sleep again for weeks.

⌒

Looking back, I placed an unfair amount of blame on Garrison Keillor for cursing me with insomnia. There were a lot of other things going on at the time that were more likely culprits, even if the Night the Boom Box Died provided a conspicuous trigger. Like the fact that I graduated from a local public elementary school where I floated along in a relatively unchallenging gifted program to a big, nearly windowless high school nicknamed the Brick Prison, where kids routinely threatened suicide when they got B's.* Or the fact that my first assignment at said high school was to write an outline of the US Constitution, which spewed out of our cutting-edge dot matrix printer on twenty-five perforated pages. Or the fact that my two closest friends at my new school had recently, after seven months of joined-at-the-hip camaraderie, informed me that I was being voted off the island.

"It's not you," Vanessa—half-Japanese and half-British, the most exotic friend I'd had to date—had said, in the gym locker room of all places, the epicenter of adolescent shame and self-loathing, as we changed out of our sweaty uniforms and back into our street clothes. "It's *us*."

---

*In 2013, it would be identified in a study as the saddest geographical spot in Manhattan.

"Yeah," piped up Jesse, a thickly accented Queens girl with crimped red hair that fell almost to her knees. "We just think you're . . . *annoying*." Their faces told me that I had always been annoying and that it was their fault for not realizing it until that moment.

"Oh," I said, trying to control the hot tears flooding my eyes. I pulled my dad's old ACLU T-shirt off over my head and crossed my elbows over my puffy, uneven breast nubs. "Okay." I forced a smile, a smile that said even *I* knew I was annoying; I had been in on it the whole time! That's my whole thing, what makes me special. I'm so annoying that no one wants to associate with me!

After Vanessa and Jesse broke up with me, I glommed on to the only other group of girls in my homeroom, a mix of Chinese and Korean Americans and one token Indian who were blanketly referred to as "the Asian Clique." I fit right in. I vaguely remember wandering behind them in the hallways and sitting with them at lunch, inserting myself into conversations without being invited. I was so determined not to be alone that I accepted what was essentially an adjunct friendship. But even that was quickly terminated.

They left a note in my backpack a few weeks later. It was a one-page, unsecret burn book, with quotes each of them had come up with to express how obnoxious and unwelcome my presence in the Asian Clique really was. I found it while having lunch with my mom, so I couldn't pretend it didn't happen. I just started talking really fast, the naked despair acting like a whippet of helium that carried me home on a weird, desperate high. I twitched through another sleepless night, this time on a futon in my parents' room despite their protests that I was too old; I needed to hear them creak and breathe to remind me that I wasn't entirely unwanted. That I belonged somewhere. The next day at school, Marina—the Indian girl—approached me in the hallway. She had a thick, wavy triangle of hair and stick-thin arms that poked out of the gaping sleeves of her shirt like two brown Twizzlers.

"Hi," she said gently. "Did you get our note?"

In the decades since she posed this question, I've come up with a lot of things I wish I'd said in response. Most of them are some variation on "Yeah, I did, and you can go fuck [yourself/your mother/some uncomfortable inanimate object]." In some versions I just slap her, hard, and say, with a cocked eyebrow, "There. You can go give the others their share of that." (I modified and stole that line from the original *Parent Trap* starring Hayley Mills.)

But in that moment I was just a thirteen-year-old with a glitter retainer and one eyebrow, struggling to hold on to a single shred of dignity to carry me until it was time to go home and weep into my comforter, so instead I shrugged and just whispered, "Yeah. It's okay."

It was almost exactly at this point in time that I began fantasizing regularly about having action movie–style revenge battles set to popular hip-hop songs. My favorite scenario involved a public, mixed martial arts display while "Jump Around" by House of Pain blared in the background from Radio Raheem's boom box from *Do the Right Thing*. During this battle I faced off with each of my ex-friends, one by one, executing gravity-defying roundhouse kicks and capoeira moves until they ran off crying or were knocked unconscious. In my fantasies I also had glowing, blemish-free skin, straight teeth, and really good hair, and my flattering Spandex bodysuit never developed sweat stains.

My Other Top Five Fantasies, Age Thirteen

1. I have my first kiss, following an impassioned performance of Madonna's "Crazy for You," preferably set at an unchaperoned party at which I am brooding attractively in a corner and wearing the sparkly purple velvet two-piece formal outfit my mother got me for Christmas that I will later realize looks like something RuPaul might wear to impersonate Prince.

2. My first kiss, as outlined above, is with Jonathan Brandis,

after we bond over our shared birthday and how many times I have seen the movie *Ladybugs*.

3. I run into Heather Locklear at the bodega near my house where I spend all my allowance money on expired Hostess products, and I punch her right in her perfect little face, because *Billy and Allison 4eva!*

4. Circumstances conspire for me to sing an a cappella rendition of Mariah Carey's runaway hit "Emotions" before an assembly of my peers, and in addition to hitting notes only dogs can hear, I am wearing the holy grail of sexy '90s clothing, which is overalls over a striped boatneck top.

5. Someday, I learn to properly insert a tampon.

Now that I'm an adult, I'm happy to report everything is so much easier. Friends don't have to leave notes in your bag telling you how much they hate you; they can simply show their contempt by refusing to "like" your Facebook statuses. I'm much more dexterous with my cursing, and I've rekindled my romance with Gary through podcasts that I listen to while doing the dishes. However, despite my relative happiness I continue in adulthood to aspire to unreachable goals.

My Top Five Fantasies, Age Thirty-Three

1. I have a private salon in my home, staffed entirely by sassy middle-aged women with big hair who look like they stepped out of a John Waters movie. Every morning, they shampoo, condition, and style me while we discuss the previous evening's new TV episodes and eat scones.

2. Lorne Michaels overhears me doing my impression of Zooey Deschanel's Cotton commercials in line at Starbucks and decides to make me head writer for *SNL*, but I only work two afternoons a week, and obviously never Saturday nights because, hello, I have a child.

3. At wedding receptions, when one of those big circles forms, I nonchalantly dance into the center and jump through my own leg.

4. This book becomes an international bestseller. Both Louis C.K. and Barack Obama send me personal notes. I am instantly offered a Tootsie Roll endorsement campaign. *Entertainment Weekly* shoots a cover featuring me, Lena Dunham, and Tina Fey with the headline "Una! Lena! Tina!" and there is an invisible fan blowing our hair back, and I am in the middle, doing an openmouthed laugh, and someone has Photoshopped my teeth.

5. I remember to mail the rent more than eight hours prior to its being due.

I also still prefer to resolve emotional conflicts through imagined musical performances instead of confrontation. I've moved on from Madonna, but it's debatable whether I've moved on from my adolescent yearning to be accepted. After an online magazine rejected a few of my pitches recently, I minimized my e-mail window, closed my eyes, and placed myself in a dark karaoke bar, sipping Manhattans alongside elite media types like David Remnick, Adam Moss, Jill Abramson, and Maureen Dowd. As they all watched with rapt attention, I walked slowly to the front of the room, picked up a wireless microphone, and launched into a performance of Salt-N-Pepa's 1993 single "Shoop," not even pausing my technically flawless Running Man when Arianna Huffington fainted from shock at my perfect rap stylings.

These frequent daydreams have caused a new fear to take root in my gut. Maybe the truth, after all these years, is that I don't really want revenge on anyone, not even if it means I can pretend to know capoeira. I don't really wish I had told Marina to go fuck a cactus, because that's not who I am. I'm not especially brave, and I'm much quicker thinking on paper than in person. When insulted, my go-to move is still to nod and smile and then either burst into tears or say something bitchy about the person to someone else. Maybe it's not the retribution I seek, or even the chance to showcase my sweet dance moves in front of my professional idols. Maybe what I really want . . . is just the applause.

After all, I *have* always wanted to be discovered in a supermarket. I mean that like "noticed by a movie scout and propelled to international fame and fortune so that I can give charming and self-deprecating interviews to *Entertainment Weekly*," not like "discovered in the produce aisle sitting in an igloo made of toilet paper rolls after having gone missing." (But honestly, at my age, I'd take either one.)

And that really lets me off the hook, because being discovered takes absolutely no action on my part. I just have to sit back and wait for it to happen. Maybe fame will find me on the playground, as I gesture theatrically at my son in an attempt to make him stop licking a nearby tree. Maybe it will find me at the drugstore, trying to rationalize the purchase of a hundred-dollar pore-cleansing device that resembles a circular saw. There's no way of knowing, really.

Life is a mystery.

PLACES I CAN NEVER GO BACK TO, AND WHY

My friend Abby's parents' house, Austin, Texas
Soiled underpants at age eight during a sleepover, balled
them up, and hid them behind the living room couch.

*Drugstore, Seventh Avenue near Union Street, Brooklyn,
New York*
In 1996, on a routine makeup run, was with my friend
Adri when she loudly farted and then knocked over
a display case of reading glasses.

*Dry cleaner's, Flatbush Avenue and Prospect Place, Brook-
lyn, New York*
Dropped off dry cleaning circa 2004, couldn't pay for it
for four months, shame spiraled, gave up.

*Dry cleaner's, Church Street and Chambers Street, New
York, New York*
Dropped off dry cleaning in 2008, left it for two weeks,
building burned to the ground.

*Dentist's office, Washington Square West, New York, New
York*
After my last cleaning in late 2010, my longtime dentist
passed away unexpectedly. I honor his memory by
not replacing him, and by filling my own cavities with
gnarled remnants of (Sugar-Free!) Coffee Nips.

*Coffee shop, Fifth Avenue and Park Place, Brooklyn, New
York*
Ordered decaf latte, realized I forgot my wallet, told
barista I would go to an ATM, ran home and stress-
watched *Homeland* instead.

Death Becomes Me

I don't know if this is normal, but in my daily life I regularly imagine gruesome tragedies happening to me. For instance, running down the subway steps, which I always do—because you never know when the New York City subway trains are going to start approaching *stealthily*—makes me picture myself slipping and falling and belly-flopping onto the concrete, breaking a few teeth and maybe a collarbone. Or sometimes my heart will skip a beat for no reason and I'm convinced I'm experiencing sudden cardiac death—basically a fatal heart attack in a seemingly healthy person—which strikes 325,000 people a year and which, as soon as I read about it, I became convinced would happen to me. All the joy has long since gone from smoking anything—while I ended my affair with cigarettes almost a decade ago, I still lie in bed at night, imagining the tumor growing in my lung—and the one time I tried cocaine, in college, the line I chopped was as loose and thin as a frayed cobweb, since I was too afraid to end up gushing blood from my nose and seizing up like Uma Thurman in *Pulp Fiction* (yes, I know, that was heroin, but *she* thought it was coke and *she* was a drug addict, so you tell me, what are *my* odds?). I don't ride a bike often—only once a presidential term or so—but what should be a joyride turns morbid as I whiz down a rolling hill without a helmet, remembering some news story I've read about a guy whose front wheel popped off and who ended up needing a face transplant.

When I get squeamish over the imaginary bloodshed, I like to switch it up and fantasize about funerals. Sometimes it's someone very close to me who has died, but usually it's me. This fantasy almost invariably takes place while listening to music. I actually have a playlist named "Make Yourself Cry," and it gets the job done—I let the swells of soft alt-rock bring tears to my eyes, and then I snap out of it, partially because killing off loved ones for emotional masturbation fodder is in incredibly poor taste and partially because I realize that everyone on the subway platform is looking at me.

⌒

The first time I thought seriously about death I was four years old. It was at what is now the Rose Planetarium, one of the buildings that make up the Museum of Natural History, on Eighty-First Street in Manhattan. The museum was—and still is—one of my favorite places. As a kid, I just got the biggest kick out of everything about it: the taxidermied animals in their hand-painted tableaus, like weird, retro snow globes; the long, ornate staircase railings with golden lions' heads at the ends that just *begged* to be slid down; the cultural exhibits in which carefully crafted dummies representing Eskimos and Native Americans crouched over fires and modeled the latest seventeenth-century fashions, breasts and testes scandalously akimbo. My favorite exhibit, though, was the Hall of North American Mammals. I didn't go, like most girls my age, for the delicate mountain goats or the adorable flying squirrel. No, I lived for the Hall of North American Mammals because that was where my beloved Alaskan musk ox lived.

If you're unfamiliar with the musk ox, the plaque at the museum introduces them thusly:

A herd of musk oxen hunkers down to wait out a snow-storm. When the weather gets foul, their strategy is to stay and cope. Unlike Arctic caribou, musk oxen do not migrate seasonally. Instead, their squat, woolly bodies limit heat loss, even when temperatures plunge below −40°F (−40°C).

Extreme shifts in climate, however, can distress musk oxen. But this too is part of their survival strategy. Study of ancient DNA reveals that over many millennia, musk ox populations have undergone repeated boom and bust cycles in response to climate fluctuations. Being able to rebound after population collapses may have helped musk oxen survive the end of the Ice Age when most other large mammals, like woolly mammoths, died out.

Sexy, right? I can't explain why the musk ox earned my deepest affections. There are two of them in the museum's display: shape-less giants resembling supersize, dreadlocked guinea pigs (and, according to the plaque, probably smelling like patchouli). The musk oxen have long snouts, cloven hooves, and moplike brown hair that hangs to their knees. They have thick horns that swoop down and out, thinning at the ends and giving the effect of a handlebar mustache worn as a hat. If you look closely you can see little insects burrowing in the oxen's matted fur. They look out from their bleak, wintry scene with a mix of apathy and misery, and I imagine that if they had voices they would sound just like Eeyore from *Winnie-the-Pooh*: *Might as well just keep walking. Nothing to see here.* They are not cuddly or sanitary, and yet I treated them like they were my own homely, petrified pets, visiting them as often as my parents let me. I don't think I internalized that they were, in fact, lifeless skins affixed to plaster casts, but in retrospect I wonder if my obsession with the musk ox wasn't kind of a red flag that I had inherited my parents' macabre obsession with death.

I can't remember what my mother and I saw at the planetarium that day in 1984, but my pediatric clinical depression struck halfway through the show, mostly because I wasn't paying attention. I was staring up at the vast black "sky" littered with stars when I started to think about how the stars must be feeling. (This was right around the time that I stopped eating Cheerios because I imagined them screaming in anticipation of a horrible death each time I raised my spoon.) It must be lonely being a star, I decided. Lonely and incredibly boring. This triggered what was probably my first existential panic attack. Did being dead mean that you were condemned to float forever in a sea of infinite blackness, the planets revolving around you while you had nothing to do but think about how bored you were and miss Earth and your mom and your friends and Kraft macaroni and cheese?

"How did you like it?" my mother asked after the show as we walked back into daylight.

"It made me think of death," I reported solemnly. That was our last visit for a while.

⌒

By the time I was eleven, I had developed more than a passing interest in the morbid and macabre. I quickly dispensed with the Baby-sitters Club series in favor of Stephen King—my favorite was *It*, the one in which a murderous clown tears the limbs off children. In the sixth grade I wrote what I thought of as a novel, clocking in at forty-two handwritten pages, which told the story of a detective whose daughter is kidnapped by his ex-girlfriend. After a long, cross-continental chase, the spurned lover leaps off the Eiffel Tower clutching the missing girl. They both die. *The end*. Quite proud of myself, I gave it to my teacher to read (in retrospect, being a thick-necked, gold-jewelry-wearing Jerseyite with a *Welcome Back, Kotter* afro, perhaps he was not in my target audience), and he returned it with a look that—while I didn't recognize it at the time—I now understand is reserved for people on the subway wearing underpants made of tinfoil.

Looking back at my childhood it's not too hard to see where I got my penchant for morbidity. My parents were lovers of life who talked and laughed loudly, ate and drank with abandon, and kissed in public. But every time a vacation rolled around and they were leaving on a trip without us, they turned into angels of doom.

"We'll be gone for a week," my mom would say to me and my sister, zipping up her suitcase, "and we'll be taking two long international flights over vast expanses of water, probably with inexperienced pilots. So, God forbid, if the plane should go down, we've left letters and detailed instructions for both of you." We received this same speech like clockwork every time one or both parents traveled anywhere that wasn't immediately visible from our house.

"There's a blank check in an envelope in my sock drawer," my dad would whisper to us before getting into the cab waiting to take them to Penn Station. "You can drain my account. There's not much, but it should keep you afloat for a few months at least."

My sister and I read the letters the summer we were twelve and eighteen, respectively, while our parents were away on a European trip. His was titled, rather whimsically, "After"; hers was simply addressed to us. In addition to saying good-bye, my father had left specific instructions about his memorial service, including a music playlist. My mother, along with her heartfelt letter, had left contact information for their mortgage broker and how to turn off the boiler.

"What a downer," I said to my sister, riffling through a sock drawer for loose bills. "I didn't know we would still have to pay for the house."

The upper-middle-class Brooklyn neighborhood where we grew up was in many ways a privileged bubble, but it wasn't impenetrable to death. When I was thirteen, my best friend's father died of a cancerous tumor. The same year, one of Zoe's friends' mothers suffered an aneurysm that killed her instantly; later, another classmate became an orphan when both of her parents met premature accidental deaths. For the entirety of 1993, my sister took to ending every conversation with the plea "Don't die." Eventually she stopped saying it, but then she took to putting up posters of George H. W. Bush in her bedroom, which my parents and I found far more sinister.

My first major death was my paternal grandfather's, who passed away when I was seventeen. I wasn't especially close to him, but I loved him the way you automatically love the people you're related to: passively but matter-of-factly. He used to keep Life Savers Popsicles in his freezer for me and my sister when we'd visit, and every summer he'd drive us around in his big white Cadillac and let us wear one of his golf caps from an impressive collection he kept on the dash. In 1991, the day after Christmas, he had an aortal aneurysm while playing cards at the Knights of Columbus. He beat the odds and survived, only to have another aneurysm a few years later on the same day. He recovered yet again, and even though he'd since had a stroke and was confined to a wheelchair, by the time he died I'd started to think of him as invincible.

He passed away just after midnight on New Year's, capping off a seven-day stretch that would later come to be known in our family as LaMarche Death Week. I had committed to doing a midnight run with a friend in Prospect Park. We ran three miles, finishing right at twelve, and then watched the fireworks. I spent the night at my friend's house, and my sister called me the next morning to tell me the news. I didn't cry, although true to form I did try to force it. As I walked home I concentrated hard on feeling grief, but it didn't work. I felt bad that I couldn't make the tears happen, not even at his wake or funeral a few days later. When we lowered my grandfather's body into the ground, into one half of a shared plot, the other half of which was reserved for his extremely Catholic spinster girlfriend, my uncle Jerry muttered, "Phil's finally gonna get laid by Claire."

I put a letter into his coffin before we buried it, along with a flyer for my high school's production of *West Side Story*, in which I had a bit part as a sassy Puerto Rican gang member. After the funeral, my family and I walked back to the car with my grandmother. We sat silently for a while until Grandma finally spoke. "Zoe," she said, addressing my eleven-year-old sister, and I anticipated some gentle lesson about death and grief. Instead, she shook her head and said, "Those are the ugliest shoes I have ever seen."

Eight months later, packing for college, I finally cried. I was listening to, of all things, the soundtrack to *Boogie Nights*, and "Sister Christian" by Night Ranger came on. Something about the lyrics and the sad, slow melody flipped a switch and I started to sob, collapsing onto my half-packed suitcase. Now, whenever I listen to that song I well up, not just because of Grandpa Phil but also because fucking Night Ranger makes me cry, which is so incredibly lame.

⌒

While the oft-threatened plane crash never came, both of my parents (now divorced but no less insane) have continued to fetishize death in their own ways. My father does it sort of unconsciously, in his everyday decision-making. This is a man who is prone to wandering into intersections without looking up from his iPhone, and who once sent me a video he shot while riding his bike through midtown traffic. He has also been hit by a van while biking, walked into a glass wall at an ATM, and, once, more seriously, developed a lung ailment that led to a year-long investigation that maddeningly yielded no conclusive diagnosis, even after a stay at a specialty hospital in Denver. Despite being the more likely of the two to imminently perish, he has not revised his death letter as far as I know, which worries me, not least because his song selections were made in an era when Hammer pants were still considered high fashion.

My mother is more obsessed, and thus more prepared. Every so often—once a day or so—she'll remind me that either one of us could die at any minute. For instance, I have a key to a safe-deposit box that she opened at a local bank for the express purpose of my using it to collect her valuables, should she expire unexpectedly. And now that I have a kid, she worries about my safety much more than she used to.

"Didn't I promise Mommy was going to come back?" she cooed at him after a recent babysitting stint. "Didn't I?" Then she turned to me, her face darkening. "I shouldn't promise that," she scolded herself. "What if something happened to you? Then I'd be lying."

"I think he'll forgive you," I joked.

"It would traumatize him forever," she said, her eyes far-off with a look I immediately recognized as the somber excitement of a hypothetical funeral arrangement fantasy.

I took a deep breath. I had thought about it, a lot actually. I mainly worried about two things: (1) could my child survive on his own in our apartment for the ten hours or so it might take for someone to find him alone with my lifeless body? and (2) if he did survive, would the experience of being trapped alone with my corpse while Raffi played on an endless loop turn him into a Dexter-style serial killer? But I decided not to take my mother's bait.

"Actually," I said slowly, "I take comfort in the fact that if something *did* happen to me, Sam would be surrounded by family who would love and take care of him. I know he would be okay."

My mom smiled weakly and put her hand on mine. "Oh, no, dear," she said. "Trust me. He'd never recover."

Although I've given it a lot of thought since my visit to the planetarium, I still can't decide what I think happens when we die. I am forced to make it up, seeing as my family has traditionally shunned all religions that might provide some guidance on afterlife expectations. Ideally, I'd like to go to a sort of custom-made heaven that has all the things I like (cable TV, Spanish wine, Tootsie Rolls, fluffy down comforters, Gary Cooper) and none of the things I don't (fluorescent lights, the Eagles, paper cuts, volleyball). I would be able to hang out with the fellow dead for company and be reunited with people and animals who'd predeceased me, like the grandmother I never met or the stray dog I adopted in 1985 only to have him picked up by his owners a few days later. And then, whenever I wanted, I could peek in on people back on Earth—watch my children grocery shop or browse the latest exhibits at the Met. I hope I get to haunt people, too—people who were mean to me.

Or maybe, if I'm lucky, I'll end up behind glass in a diorama like my beloved musk ox. There should be a Taxidermy box you can check off when you renew your driver's license, next to Organ Donor. In my will, I'll demand that some diligent curator set me up on a replica of my couch, the coffee table in front of me spread with *Star* magazines and half-finished Sunday *New York Times* crossword puzzles. The television must be frozen on an image of Tim Gunn's face from *Project Runway* and in my hand will be a burrito, the contents of which will spill onto my Christmas print pajamas, even though the plaque in front of my diorama will specify that it is actually mid-April. It will go on to say:

> *A lone Una hunkers down to drink while watching reality television. Unlike more adventurous* Homo sapiens, *during its life the Una generally preferred to stay within a one-mile radius of its apartment. Its name is derived from the reported (and photographically confirmed) unibrow it*

was born with and later removed from its squat, woolly body. The Una can weigh over one hundred pounds, but appear much larger because of its oversize baggy pajamas.

Extreme shifts in climate and the cancellation of favorite sitcoms distressed the Una, leading to its extinction in the mid-twenty-first century. The last Una expired after experiencing sudden cardiac death brought on by hysterical weeping to the power ballad "Sister Christian" by Night Ranger, an American rock band that gained popularity during the 1980s and then faded into obscurity.

AFTER

When I Die:

1. Delete my browser history.

2. Send out the news to all my contacts in a classy way, i.e., Paperless Post, not Evite.

3. Start a letter-writing campaign to get Uma Thurman to change her name out of respect.

4. Book an auditorium and a gospel choir with at least a few members who can do backflips. In lieu of flowers, please remind people to bring individually wrapped six-packs of Little Debbie Frosted Donettes to toss into my cremation urn.

5. Prepare a slideshow of flattering photographs of me (*nothing between 1992 and 1999—I am serious, Mom*) in which I look impossibly fresh and happy and alive with pleasure. So basically a Virginia Slims ad, but without the cigarettes. (Any shots with bongs, joints, or enormous vats of liquor should also be removed.)

6. While playing slideshow, have gospel choir perform "Joyful, Joyful" as seen at the end of *Sister Act 2: Back in the Habit*. Please retain as much of the original choreography and 1993 wardrobe choices as possible.

7. Once service is completed, please mail the box of pre-addressed and stamped envelopes that I have prepared for guests with whom I have unfinished emotional business. (You may have to add extra postage depending on inflation rates. If the Postal Service has folded, please arrange for delivery by drone.)

8. Erect statue in my likeness in a peaceful area unfrequented by pigeons, rats, or mimes. Position my body so that tourists will want to pose with me but not in a lewd way.

9. Check to make sure you *really* deleted my browser history.

10. You know what, just burn my computer.

HOMEMADE SELF-DEFENSE WEAPONS

"The Wolverine," aka "The Deadly Janitor"

Materials Needed:

- 1 ring of way too many keys, half of which open doors you no longer have legal access to

Instructions:

1. Hold key ring in palm of dominant hand.
2. Stick keys in between fingers.
3. Clench fist so that keys protrude like claws.
4. Maul attackers.

"The Freelancer's Revenge"

Materials Needed:

- 1 Ziploc bag or unmatched sock
- Anywhere from five to sixty dollars in coins
- Procrastination

Instructions:

1. Run out of money.
2. Fill a Ziploc bag (or, for purists, a sock) with all the loose change you can find in your house.
3. Put off going to the bank to cash them in, partially out of laziness but mostly out of the shame you will be faced with upon sidling up to the Penny Arcade (or, worse, an actual teller).
4. Beat mugger unconscious with sack of useless legal tender.

"The Abandoned Master Cleanse"

Materials Needed:

- Purified water
- Grade B maple syrup
- Fresh-squeezed lemon juice
- Cayenne pepper
- Lack of willpower
- Spray bottle

Instructions:

1. Resolve to do the Master Cleanse, in which you subsist for days on nothing but water mixed with lemon juice, cayenne pepper, and "grade B" maple syrup—whatever that is—in order to rid your body of a lifetime of accumulated toxins, including but not limited to the Taco Bell Doritos Locos Cheesy Gordita Crunch, grain alcohol, and swallowed gum.
2. Give up after two hours; eat a hamburger.
3. Siphon remaining Master Cleanse juice into small spray bottle; store in purse or jacket pocket.
4. Upon encountering menace, spray into eyes and nostrils.
5. As you run, remind him/her that the burn means it's working!

Sissy Fuss

Every single day I set my alarm for seven a.m. And every single morning I snooze for another hour or so—usually until my toddler kicks me in the face to signal the fact that morning has arrived. Why do I torture myself day after day with interrupted sleep? I'm glad you asked. It's because I believe, deep in my soul, that one day—soon! tomorrow, probably!—I will bound out of bed, fresh and flush with health, and finally do some exercise.

This never happens. I would say that my quest for physical fitness is Sisyphean, but Sisyphus actually pushed a giant boulder up a hill, which, if you take a look at my biceps, is obviously not something I could do. Also, Zeus was punishing him for being a sly and gossipy murderer, and I'm only being punished by myself, for eating too much pad thai. My main problem is that I want to be toned but don't want to work at it; to paraphrase Ethan Hawke in *Reality Bites*, I am the reason the Ab Rocket was invented.

I have gone to extraordinarily lazy extremes to stave off the letting-myself-go process. I own a pair of phenomenally expensive sneakers that look like orthopedic platforms and are designed to work my calves and butt while I am standing or walking. I think they work, but I can't actually tell because they are so ugly that I have to wear long pants with them, thus hiding my legs. I also own a Pilates magic circle, which looks like a giant, flexible intrauterine device and which is used to build muscle through resistance exercises. It's a glorified ThighMaster, but I happily trot it out during commercials, doing pliés until it inevitably springs from my knees and flies across the room and breaks something.

Once upon a time, I belonged to a gym. Actually, technically it's *thrice* upon a time, since I managed to join and quit three different gyms. I do not like going to the gym—I don't like waiting for machines or being self-conscious about my ratty gym clothes or attempting to shower behind a tissue-thin curtain that does not go all the way to the wall on either side—but I am vain, so for a long time I figured a gym membership was a necessary evil if I wanted to keep fit. My first gym, right out of college, turned out to be too expensive to afford on my nonexistent salary. The next one was cheap but too far from home, so I never went. Then I got a job that came with a free gym membership. And it all would have worked out beautifully if it wasn't for Clive, a sexy personal trainer who approached me on my first day and coerced me into spending twelve hundred dollars on a dozen sessions. (By "coerced," of course, I mean "asked me if I wanted to," as I am incapable of saying no to anyone, ever. Especially if they look like a black John Krasinski.) I charged the sessions on a credit card and stocked up on ramen noodles for the coming famine. I have to admit that during those three months, I loved the gym. I looked forward to my workout each week, especially the stretching part when Clive would lean on me and push my legs back over my head. When my sessions ran out Clive assumed I would sign up for more, but I couldn't tell him that I was broke, so I quit the gym to avoid him. He called me once to try to change my mind and I lied and said I'd lost my job.

Since I can no longer show my face at any gyms in the metropolitan New York area, over the years I have amassed a small library of fitness DVDs. Jeff calls the stash my "porn," which is inaccurate—if they actually *were* porn I would watch them way more often. As it is I only use a few—the ones that require the least effort on my part. It's telling that my favorite video is *The Girls Next Door Workout*, which stars three of Hugh Hefner's former Playboy Mansion girlfriends. The ladies' buoyant chests and tight outfits prevent them (and, by extension, me) from doing anything too strenuous, and their shining, Barbie-blond pigtails and bright smiles lull me into a trance so deep that I barely realize I'm moving.

A few years ago I also purchased Nintendo's Wii Fit, mostly because it seemed like the perfect workout regimen for someone who needs to be distracted (in this case, by a video game) in order to exercise. Unfortunately, after only a few uses I was forced by vanity to shove the system under the couch and cower in fear. For instance, no one had told me that if I did not use it every single day, the Wii would chide me as soon as I started. "Oh, too busy to work out yesterday?" it would mock in a high-pitched, childlike voice not unlike *2001: A Space Odyssey*'s HAL after a few hits of helium. I don't know about you, but standing in front of my TV wearing a sports bra is a vulnerable position for me. Being mocked in that state sends me into the kitchen for some ice cream and/or vodka. Also, before each exercise, the Wii would ask me to step onto a balance board so that it could weigh me and register my alignment. For some reason, half the time when I stepped on, the voice would say, "Okay!" but the other half of the time it would exclaim, "Oh!" Like, "Oh! Wow! We've got a big'un! Send in the reinforcements!" A year and about a dozen workouts after I bought it, I sold the Wii Fit for half of what I paid, and used the profits to purchase an iTunes Season Pass to *Living Lohan*.

Oprah Winfrey is famous for her "aha! moments," flashes of enlightenment or emotional breakthroughs, which the big O seems to have with the regularity that most people move their bowels. I've had my very own aha! moment. In the fall of my senior year of high school I realized how much I hated fitness and how far I was willing to go to avoid it.

On that fateful day, I was sitting on the uptown 1 train to Van Cortlandt Park in the Bronx, reluctantly on my way to a cross-country track meet. As usual, I was terrified.

Simply put, I hated track. I hated everything about it. I hated running, for starters. I hated competition. I hated stripping down to my flimsy purple short shorts—seemingly cut so as to enhance and encourage saddlebag jigglage—in the chill of November and waiting for the gun to go off to signal the start of the race. I hated feeling my lungs burn and my hamstrings cramp and swallowing my own coppery saliva. I hated the way my legs went all rubbery as I neared the finish line, reducing me to the speed and acuity of a milk-drunk toddler. Most of all I hated the actual running part. Sitting on that subway train, filled with dread, I realized I had to do something to get myself out of the race—and off the team—for good.

I had only joined track in the first place because my friend Rachel convinced me it would be a good character-building exercise. Up until sophomore year, my extracurricular activities had been limited to art club and a local musical theater class composed mostly of twelve-year-olds. I had the pasty, black-and-white complexion of Peter Lorre in *M*. Rachel, by comparison, was almost six feet tall and built like a tree. She played a different sport every season. She glowed with health. I don't know what I was thinking, listening to her. I guess I hoped that running would change me as a person. I clung to the belief that it might sprout me up a few inches, turn my chalk-colored skin a healthy peach, and form sinewy muscles out of the soft, fatty pads of my calves and upper arms, which were so undeveloped that neighbors probably suspected that my parents were raising me for veal.

I should have known that I was kidding myself. Genetically—and I'm certain this could be backed up by a blood test—I am at an athletic disadvantage compared to most of the world's population. I come from a family that has churned out successful musicians, businesspeople, artists, and writers, but put up a volleyball net at one of our reunions and you'd think someone had called in a bomb threat. It is a true story that my father, who was captain of his high school debate team, once put his back out changing a roll of toilet paper. I was never forced (or even encouraged) to play competitive sports as a kid, but somehow I must have intuited my lack of ability because I soon came to live in fear of them. As early as first grade, I used to make myself physically ill over whether I would have gym class on any given day. To calm my nerves, I'd make my dad ask my teacher about gym day when he dropped me off. On one memorable occasion, after she said no and I relaxed as my father turned to leave, Ms. McHenry corrected herself.

"I'm sorry, Mr. LaMarche," she said, "I was wrong; Una does have gym today."

I promptly burst into tears.

⁓

When my family moved to New York and I started at a new elementary school, my fledgling fear became more of an acute phobia. Suddenly I had two gym teachers: Mr. Hyman—short, stocky, white, and loud, with reddish hair that matched his constantly flushed face—and Mr. Bolden—tall, muscular, reticent, and black, with heavy-lidded eyes and an ever-present basketball wedged in the crook of his elbow. They were always together, sort of like Ernie and Bert crossed with Riggs and Murtaugh from *Lethal Weapon*. Twice a week, our class would file into the gym in our maroon-and-urine-accented uniforms and sit cross-legged in rows.

The games Hyman and Bolden forced us to play ran the gamut from farcical to torturous. Sometimes we'd push a giant beach ball across the room for no reason; other days they had us doing timed sprints around the school yard or hanging limply from the chin-up bar as Mr. Hyman barked, "Don't just hang there; pull! Use your arms, for Christ's sake." The one sport I wasn't completely embarrassing at was something called scooter soccer, a game seemingly designed to handicap everyone. The essential rules of soccer were the same, except that instead of standing or running, we sat on little squares of plastic with wheels. Since this was public school in the 1980s, the wheels were often warped and in order to move at all we had to pound the floor furiously while pushing backward. In retrospect I liked it not so much because I was good at it, but because no one else was.

But as terrified as I was of gym pretty much all the time, I was never more nervous than on the days that we played a game Mr. Hyman called "basketball." For the record, it wasn't basketball. As athletically challenged as I am, I *know* how basketball is played. (Sort of.) No, this was what basketball would have been in *Lord of the Flies*—a sudden-death gauntlet aimed at weeding out the uncoordinated. The class was divided into teams and counted off so that everyone had a nemesis on the opposite side of the gym with the same number. Two basketballs were placed in the center of the floor, and we crouched on either side, some literally vibrating with excitement, others just willing our bladders to be strong. Mr. Hyman would stand at the front of the room and shout in his thick New York accent—*"Numbaaaaaaaaaaah...five!"*—and immediately two kids would sprint to the center, grab the basketballs, and start shooting for the basket. At that time I was less than five feet tall, weighed about sixty pounds, and had truly horrible aim. My utter failure wouldn't have been so humiliating if not for the fact that we were not allowed to sit back down—even if the competition had made their shot on the first try—until we made a basket. I would stand there for what felt like hours, heaving the ball with both hands toward the net, sometimes missing even the backboard.

The cruelest part, looking back, was that I was too young to know that Hyman was a funny last name.* I know it probably wouldn't have changed anything that came after, but I still like to imagine my skinny, prematurely hairy adolescent self spinning on her Reebok high-top-clad heel and dropping her basketball with a dramatic sneer, saying, "Yeah, I suck at basketball. But at least my last name isn't part of a *vagina*." Then all my classmates would slow clap. (Incidentally, slow clapping during fantasy revenge monologues is probably my best adult sport.)

⌒

Fast-forward to high school, two awkward gym uniforms, and one retainer later. Seeing as my hands and eyes were still about as coordinated as an epileptic busboy's, and since I had Rachel as my enabler, I decided that track was my only option if I was ever going to get into something as wholesome as extracurricular organized sports. The big selling point for me was that the sole requirement for eligibility was the ability to remain upright while moving forward. To excel, of course, you had to be strong and fast, but to be a member of the team all you had to do was show up. My high school was a magnet school for math and science and attracted the types of kids who begged Santa for new graphing calculators. Jocks were in short supply.

It didn't take long for me to realize I had made a mistake. On my very first day I had to run a timed loop of the Central Park Reservoir—just over a mile and a half—under the supervision of the coach, whom I'll call Ms. Patchman. (I'm changing her name because I'm sure I'm about to exaggerate her awfulness—she scared me so much that she lives in my memory as a cartoonish killjoy, some cross between Nurse Ratched and Clint Eastwood in

---

*My computer teacher at the same school was Ms. Klitnick. Coincidence or hiring policy?

Million Dollar Baby.) Ms. Patchman was tiny but imposing. Scrawny and shriveled, she wore her hair in a close-cropped, wispy Afro the color of rusty tap water. I had heard rumors around school that she was a "lesbo," but she did not seem to like girls, or anyone, for that matter. Me especially.

When I arrived at the reservoir entrance, she narrowed her eyes and nodded once in weary acknowledgment of my presence. "Ever run this far?" she asked. I mumbled that I had not. She considered this for a moment and then sighed. "If you vomit," she finally said, "try to do it off the main path." I like to think that it's to my credit that I didn't throw up until I got home that night.

I started group practice the following day and found that there was safety in numbers. Running with the rest of the team allowed me to study and imitate them, as if I were doing field research on an alien race. There were a few slower girls I could keep pace with, and I carefully pumped my arms and kicked my legs along with them. I learned how to run through a "stitch" by pinching the muscle and breathing deeply, and even if I didn't have one I would mime one every so often just to seem legit to the Japanese tourists snapping photos along the reservoir path. I also learned a lot about Ms. Patchman from the other girls. Legend had it she had once been a great runner but had injured her knee and had to retire. They were all pretty sure that she didn't wear a bra, but none were willing to do the kind of research necessary to find out definitively. She had once chaperoned a school dance wearing a bolo tie and blew a whistle when kids started slow dancing to "November Rain."

Ms. Patchman kept her office in our high school's basement with the rest of the physical education teachers and encouraged us to visit for one-on-one performance reviews, but I couldn't bring myself to go. Not only was I already terrified of her, but I had also unintentionally flashed one of her colleagues, Mr. Mistriel, during an eighth-grade swim class in which I opted for a floral

cotton suit with a sweetheart neckline instead of my more trust-
worthy Speedo. I had propped myself up on the lip of the pool to
ask a question, and when I looked down I saw that the neckline
had stretched below my rib cage. The thought of accidentally running into the man who had seen my awkward, fledgling nipples
was more than I could bear.

Since I was a terrible runner, it was pretty easy to avoid interacting directly with Ms. Patchman; she spent the vast majority of
her time training and tending to the good runners on the team.
The slow runners were treated with a mix of apathy and disgust,
like we were stray cats peeing in the hay reserved for her thor-
oughbreds, and she eventually separated our workouts from those
of the varsity girls' so that we wouldn't slow them down. Not that
we minded. All of us in JV were thrilled that we hadn't raised
anyone's expectations of our abilities; in fact, we kept them low
on purpose. One spring, I accidentally won an eight-hundred-
meter race by inadvertently joining the slowest heat, made up of
the types of people who carry inhalers and wear strapped-on goggles. You should have seen Ms. Patchman's face when I crossed
the finish line—I think she almost smiled. As I collected my medal
I cursed myself for having done well enough to get her attention,
but then the next week I tripped over a hurdle and the universe
righted itself again.

Unfortunately, no amount of underachieving could exempt me
from the weekly 5K races that were part of fall's cross-country
schedule, which was how I found myself on that uptown train
senior year, my muscles tense and my stomach in knots, trying to
find a way out. A braver person would have simply marched over
to Ms. Patchman—who was sitting alone at the opposite end of
the subway car—and quit then and there, but I was too afraid. A
healthy respect for authority figures combined with a near-
evangelical devotion to conflict avoidance led me to believe that
telling my coach that I wanted to quit the track team would be like

a made man telling Vito Corleone that he wanted to stop whacking people. I fantasized about Ms. Patchman ripping my uniform off my body with her bare hands and then marching me up to the registrar's office and demanding that I be expelled. The next morning I might wake up to find a lacerated sneaker under my covers, reservoir mud seeping into my sheets, and then I'd have to change schools and use my mom's last name, and maybe even get a nose job before I'd stop having nightmares about waking to find her standing in my doorway with a starter gun aimed at my forehead.

Oprah says that an aha! moment is like a lightbulb turning on in your brain, but mine was more like a floodlight. All of a sudden I had the answer, a way to get out of running without quitting, a solution that would grant me an honorable discharge from my own personal hell.

All I had to do was to hurt myself. Badly.

The five-kilometer course at Van Cortlandt Park takes the charming shape of a dandelion blossom spilling out of a dented tin can. The start and finish lines are located a tenth of a mile or so apart on a vast expanse of balding grass known as "the Flats." The first mile is run in full view of onlookers; when the race starts, runners head south in a thick pack and make two left turns, essentially forming the bottom of a square, before veering off onto a dirt road called "the Cow Path" (named for the—surprise!—actual cows that grazed there before the Van Cortlandt family donated the land to the city). Then, mercifully, thick woods hide the beet-red faces and jiggling thighs from view as runners advance toward the more treacherous terrain of "the Back Hills."

I knew that I could not stage my fall on the open plains of the Flats or the soft incline of the Cow Path; I needed a good, steep downhill slope, preferably dotted with loose, jutting rocks and toe-catching tangles of dead branches. Ironically, the adrenaline in anticipation of my painful freedom caused me to run the first mile faster than ever, and to the casual observer I'm sure I must have looked relaxed and confident, like a really, really slow white version of Flo-Jo. Little did they know that, instead of humming the *Chariots of Fire* theme music or focusing on my breathing, I was trying to calculate the angle of impact at which I might be able to twist an ankle without actually breaking it. I wasn't after real pain and suffering, after all; I just wanted a sob story that would get me out of gym. I thought of my best friend, Anna, who as a child had coveted a friend's plaster cast so passionately that she attempted to break her own leg with a hammer. "I remember holding it in the air with both hands," she told me later, "but I just couldn't bring myself to do it." She found it easier to "accidentally" fall out of her bunk bed, but ended up with nothing more than a black eye, courtesy of a turret on her She-Ra Princess of Power Crystal Castle. She didn't even get an eye patch.

Approximately a mile and a half into the Van Cortlandt 5K course, runners come to a small, graffiti-covered footbridge that crosses over the Henry Hudson Parkway and serves as the de facto entrance into the Back Hills. On a map, the Back Hills form a rough circle that resembles a nubby, fetal fist waving hello, but on the ground they are far more menacing. (Wikipedia even calls them "infamous," and Wikipedia's seen it *all*.) The Back Hills go on for almost a mile and a half and are the last leg of the race that's run under cover of woods. So I knew that in order to carry out my plan, I had to throw myself down one of them.

I feel I should take a moment to mention here that this wasn't the first time I had tried to injure myself in an attempt to be honorably discharged from the wide world of sports. When I was eleven I joined a soccer league (possibly against my will; details remain murky). I asked my parents to let me quit the very first night, but, having already paid for cleats, knee pads, a completely unnecessary sports bra, and a nonrefundable enrollment fee, they said no. I spent the next eight weeks standing frozen on the field, refusing to move, waiting for one of the bigger kids to tackle me. I wanted nothing more than to limp home battered and bruised so that my parents—bleeding-heart liberal pacifists—would see the error of their ways and see that they had forced me into a horrifying twilight zone.

"We're supposed to *run* after a *ball*," I would report. "We're supposed to run even though no one is chasing us and there isn't a bus coming."

My mother would look up briefly from the newspaper. "Well, just pretend there is, honey."

It's one thing to passively hope to be trampled, but it takes a special mix of willpower and stupidity to actively throw yourself down a rocky incline, especially when you're wearing only a thin tank top and a pair of shorts with built-in underpants. But as I neared the final hill of that day's race my resolve grew strong. All of a sudden I *did* start to hear the *Chariots of Fire* theme as I crested the hill. I was almost free! Free of the tyranny of Patchman and her saggy breasts and dour expressions. Free from the injustice of being made to sprint without the impetus of an air raid siren or pack of rabid dogs! With visions of glory dancing through my head and mumbled apologies to my left ankle, I faltered dramatically over a branch, buckled, and went down.

It never occurred to me that I wouldn't actually hurt myself. But the moment I tripped, my arms shot out to cushion my fall, an automatic nervous system reaction that I could not will away. My palms smacked against the dirt, followed by my knees. I didn't somersault treacherously down the path; I merely went from being vertical to horizontal, like a military recruit dropping to do a push-up. My ankle was unharmed, apart from a scratch from the branch that refused, cruelly, even to break the skin. Luckily, no one knew this but me.

"Are you okay?" someone cried, and soon there was a group of girls around me, helping me up, dusting me off. I could see that they were mentally ticking off the seconds that this act of good Samaritanism would rob from their finish times, so I smiled and said I was fine, that they should go on ahead. Then, once they were out of sight, I began to limp, slowly but surely, toward the final stretch.

I lurched awkwardly out of the woods and into view of the crowds at the finish line, dragging my left ankle behind me and fixing what I hoped was a look of grim determination on my face. The first person I saw was a varsity runner from my team named Kate. Kate was barrel shaped, with calves so muscular that from behind they looked like arrows pointing down at her ankles. She was screaming so hard at the other runners that spittle flew from her lips. When she saw me, her eyes flitted from my dirty tank top to my gimpy leg, and suddenly she stopped yelling and started to clap. "Way to go, Una!" she said warmly as I passed her. "Finish strong." I smiled beatifically through my imaginary pain. This was exactly the reaction I had hoped for. Injured but persevering, I would limp my way into the hearts of all my teammates. "What a good sport that Una is," they'd say during their daily warm-ups. "Sprained her ankle but finished the race anyway. What commitment! What sportsmanship! It's too bad she's out for the rest of the season and then graduating. We'll really miss running with such a consummate athlete."

My reverie was interrupted by the sight of Ms. Patchman, watching me with binoculars from a seat on the bleachers. She looked confused as I shuffled past, parting the throng of runners like Moses, with my foot drawing a sad, squiggly line in the path behind me, but as I crossed the finish line, wincing dramatically, suddenly she appeared.

"What the hell happened?" she barked, as I searched her voice for undertones of suspicion.

"My ankle," I muttered. "I fell."

"Better have someone take a look at it," she said grimly, gesturing to a husky man pacing nearby with a roll of Ace bandages. "I can't lose you this early in the season." It might have been my imagination, but I could swear she narrowed her eyes at me just then, her hand worrying the key ring on her left hip as though we were facing off at high noon. Wincing again gave me the opportunity to narrow *my* eyes. *Oh yeah?* I drawled telepathically as tumbleweeds, in the form of leaves, blew by. *Wanna bet?*

⌒

"Tell me if this hurts," the Ace bandage guy said, pressing down on the flesh just below my ankle with his thumb. I was on my back in a makeshift tent a few yards from the finish line, alone but for one other girl who had fainted after the race and was recuperating on a nearby cot. I glared at her, her and her actual medical condition. *Bitch*, I thought. I hadn't anticipated a doctor's visit, but I wasn't willing to give up hope. I kicked myself for not having consulted a medical textbook as part of my plan. I had no idea what was supposed to hurt when you had a sprain, so I played it safe and went with everything.

"Ow!" I howled when he moved his fingers slightly upward.

"On a scale of one to ten, how much did that hurt?" he asked. I considered this for a moment. Once, as a child, I had backflipped off a porch swing and bashed my head against a concrete slab (an incident that could probably be blamed for my current situation). If it was hard enough to cause irreparable brain damage, it must have been a ten. As for my foot . . . "Um, eight?" I guessed.

"Well, there's no swelling, which is odd, but it's probably a sprain," he said. *Swell!* I silently commanded my ankle. "From the amount of pain you're in, I'd say it could be broken . . ." he continued. Oh God, no. Had I overshot? Was I headed to a hospital, where an X-ray would reveal that I was nothing more than a big, fat—and yet suspiciously unswollen—liar? "Except that (a) you're not crying and (b) you were able to walk the rest of the race," he finished. I smiled thinly.

"I just didn't want to let Ms. Patchman down," I said, fluttering my eyelids. By the time he fitted me with a temporary air cast and gave me the number of an orthopedic specialist to follow up with, I was spent. It had been the performance of a lifetime.

Later that night I allowed my parents to serve me ice cream as they elevated my foot with pillows, and later that week I faked my way through an appointment with a doctor on the Upper West Side and got another, fancier air cast, which I dutifully wore to school for the remainder of the fall semester. Apart from getting me out of track practices, the air cast granted me bleacher rest during gym class—my lifelong aspiration—as well as access to the school elevator. When I passed phys ed teachers in the hallway they nodded reverently, wordlessly acknowledging that I had, in the most literal sense of the phrase, taken one for the team. Ms. Patchman mostly ignored me once our paths stopped crossing daily, but at the end-of-the-year sports banquet, held at an Italian restaurant just before graduation, she called me up to accept an award for team spirit. I had long since abandoned the air cast by then, and the muscles I had developed running had softened to the texture of the mozzarella sticks we were shoveling into our mouths. As my teammates applauded, I rose, wiping marinara sauce from my cheek with the back of my wrist, and walked to the front of the room to accept what was a Lifetime Underachievement Award. Having spent the better part of my youth shedding sweat, tears, and fake menstrual fluids in the pursuit of athletic avoidance, I was about as qualified for a team spirit award as Keith Richards is to donate blood.

Still I took it and shook Ms. Patchman's tiny, wizened hand, and as I looked out into the crowd I thought of Ms. McHenry, Mr. Hyman, Mr. Bolden, Mr. Mistriel, and every other education professional who'd ever struck fear into my heart in the name of physical fitness. And then I had my second aha! moment, which was that I should have just quit outright, or invented a disease, and that I was nothing but an insanely passive-aggressive drama queen who couldn't remember which foot she was supposed to be limping on half the time. But I forced myself to smile, secure in the knowledge that at the very least I was headed to a college with no gym requirement. If a window into the future had opened up at that second, I would have seen myself in my dorm room, a year later and ten pounds heavier, hoisting a handle of vodka in an inadvertent biceps curl as I searched the floor for my carton of Marlboro Reds. Beyond that, I might have seen myself as a recent college graduate on the streets of New York, beginning to run for a bus but then flipping it off as it roared past me and waving for a cab instead. And beyond that, if I squinted, I might have seen myself with a bundle of kids, homeschooling them to spare them the countless athletic humiliations our genetic legacy promised, holding a big bowl of popcorn as we paused the afternoon lesson to crack open a magazine and find out what Oprah had discovered about herself that day.

Late Bloomer

I have long held a secret wish that there was some way I could see, standing in a military-style line, all the people who had ever fantasized about having sex with me. So long as no blood relatives or childhood friends' parents appeared, I always figured it would be extremely gratifying to see everyone whose world I had unwittingly rocked. On my better days I estimated there might be a few dozen; on less confident days I feared there would be no one—not even the people I'd *actually* had sex with. But then one night in early 2012, I learned the truth.

Jeff and I were out on a date. It was only the third time we'd been out without the kid since he'd been born, and so naturally we were trying to drink as much as possible before the bill arrived or we were summoned back home to an inconsolable baby, whichever came first. We were on new-parent speed, and the rush was so intoxicating that it gave us an uncharacteristic sense of abandon.

"Let's do it in the bathroom!" my normally unadventurous husband whispered as soon as the busboy had cleared our apps. "It's big and it smells like vanilla!"

Perhaps it was my refusal to engage in sink sex (I should add—and not just for my parents' benefit—that we have never done the deed in any bathroom we weren't paying rent on) that spurred his confession, two beers later, that he regretted never having slept with an Asian woman. I tried to commiserate.

"Yeah, there are a few people I wish I'd gotten the chance to sleep with."

"Like how many?"

"I don't know"—I did know; I keep a running tally—"five?"

He was shocked. Not that there were five people I still wanted to bang even though I supposedly had eyes for only him—but that my number was so low.

"Chances are," he explained between long pulls on his beer, "any woman I've met, I've at least thought about . . . what it would be like."

I was floored. "*Any* woman?"

He shrugged. "Pretty much."

I immediately blurted out the name of the least physically attractive female I could think of who had ever crossed paths with Jeff (again, running tally). "Even *her*?" I demanded.

"Now that you mention it, yeah."

I considered the ramifications of this world-shattering news. I mean, yes, sure, *When Harry Met Sally* had reported it back in 1989, but I'd always thought it only applied to uncontrollable sexual dynamos like Billy Crystal. Not to my sweet, reticent, devoted husband. How many of my friends, coworkers, and relatives had Jeff pictured in compromising positions through the years? I was about to start a fight when I saw the silver lining, glistening under the pile of writhing bodies like a discarded metallic thong.

If all men were like Jeff, then that meant they had all thought the same thing about me. In an instant, my short military line of would-be paramours became a troop a thousand strong.

⌒

Given that my first crush was a mythical centaur hybrid of Garrison Keillor and Ted Danson, you won't be surprised to learn that

I was a late bloomer. There were other indicators, too, like my troll doll earring collection and the fact that I was naturally drawn to gorgeous best friends who transformed me, by comparison, into the homely sidekick (in troll doll earrings*).

In elementary school, I stood in the shadow of Halima, a dusky Belizean beauty who was worshipped by every boy in our fifth-grade class. Girls and women like this, I have come to realize, all have one thing in common, and that is a natural shit-givinglessness that I have never and will never possess. They are confident enough in themselves that they don't need to be liked, and there-fore they are psychotically adored by all. As Halima's best friend, I enjoyed a status boost that came with name recognition but al-most no actual power—kind of like the vice president. Boys began to befriend me in an attempt to get close to her, sometimes passing me notes or presents, which I, of course, would open (one line that has stayed with me: *Halima's butt crack is long and narrow / Just one whiff makes me fly like a sparrow*). When they would inev-itably be rejected (a decade later, Halima would come out as a lesbian), I would comfort them, basking in the intimacy by proxy. "You know," a boy named Charles—whose big brown doe eyes I quietly coveted—told me one day, as we sat commiserating in the cafeteria, "if your personality was in Halima's body, you would be the perfect woman."†

"You asshole," I snapped, hitting him close-fisted in the balls. "That shitty backhanded compliment is going to haunt me for the rest of my life."

Just kidding. I think I actually said, "Thanks."

In Charles's defense, though, I don't think he knew I secretly

*You can safely assume that if you're reading about anything that hap-pened to me between 1989 and 1992, I was wearing troll doll earrings at the time. If it was December, they were dressed as Santa.

†Many years later, I would include this line in a young adult novel, and my editor would tell me it was too "on the nose" to be believable.

loved him. This was because at the time, my primary methods of flirting were as follows:

- Avoid eye, voice, or physical contact at all times.
- Wear enormous, adult-man-size Bartman T-shirt that renders body amorphous.
- Roller-skate around living room listening to Madonna's *Dick Tracy* soundtrack on Walkman, passing conspicuously by the big front windows while performing arabesques. (This makes sense only if you know Charles lived next door.)

Halima and I eventually became insufferable, because the popularity (earned by her; siphoned off by me) went to our heads and turned us into stereotypical mean girls who made fun of everyone and acted like we were—to use the terminology of that era—stupid fly. But Charles did kiss me once, on the earlobe, during a game of sixth-grade truth or dare. He was supposed to kiss me on the lips, but I turned my head at the last second.

I would not make it to first base for another four years.

MY SEXUAL HISTORY:
A GAME OF BASEBALL PLAYED BY EXTREMELY SLOW-MOVING, UNCOORDINATED FOREIGNERS FROM A COUNTRY WHERE BASEBALL DOES NOT EXIST

First Base: 1996

It took me sixteen years to kiss another (non-blood-relative) human being on the mouth for many reasons, but the main obstacle was that my fantasy world was far too rich to leave any room for actual life experience. I wanted all the thrills of obsessive lust without the risk of real vulnerability, so what I would do was essentially date people in my mind.

When I started high school, I met a cool and quirky brainiac named Anna, who remains one of my best friends to this day. Anna and I clicked immediately—as so many teenagers do—because we were mean and crazy in all the same ways. We used to sit in the back row of biology and giggle over what our sweet, matronly, hard-of-hearing teacher would say if, when prompted for the third time to speak louder, we yelled, "I *said*, GO FUCK YOURSELF!" Each of us thought the other was hilarious and totally underrated by our classmates. And we completely enabled each other's penchant for acting totally insane about boys.

I don't mean insane in the normal teenage girl way of being "boy crazy." I mean we basically acted like serial killers. We used to cut out the letters of our crushes' names, rearrange them to make anagrams, and then analyze the results. We made fortune-tellers out of loose-leaf paper and rigged them to tell us what we wanted to hear. We conspired to create scenarios in which we'd get to actually speak to the object of our desire, and we'd prepare by rehearsing the literally dozens of potential ways the conversation could play out—I'm also pretty sure we purchased voodoo dolls at one point. It was like we were playing our own version of Dungeons and Dragons, only with fewer elves and more steamy make-out scenes set in the abandoned fourth-floor computer lab.

My high school crush—whom I will call Fernando both to protect his privacy and also in the hopes that if he ever reads this he doesn't realize it's him because he's not Latino—did not actually go to my high school. He was the son of my parents' friends and I got to see him once every few months when our families would have dinner. He was *also*, conveniently, a *child actor*, so when I was really jonesing for a hit I could just go see the 1994 remake of *Lassie* over and over again in the theater, swooning as his name appeared in the opening credits. I penned a number of humiliating diary entries detailing our brief interactions as if we were the two stars of a passionately G-rated telenovela.

> *November 20, 1994*
> *"The Morning After"*
> *I don't know if I can bear it. I'm in love. Fernando is everything I want. Before, I don't think I was quite sure, but any reservations I may have had were swept away with last night. I think I have to get this out on paper or I'll burst.*
>
> *We didn't talk much for almost ten minutes. Then we started a conversation about school. Forget that now, thow [sic]. What actually mattered was later, in my room. We entered and shared the first of many uncomfortable silences. Then he saw my Beatles tapes. He said he loved the Beatles. I could have kissed him.*
>
> *I felt comfortable, but also tense. I kept wondering if he felt for me like I did for him. I put on my Minnie Mouse ears. He loved them. I loved that he loved them.*
>
> *We lay on my bed together (!!) and pet Fifi for a while.*

Every few minutes there would be a moment of silence and,
as far as I could tell, sexual tension. I savored those mo-
ments. Sometimes our hands would touch when we were
petting Fifi, and he complimented my haircut.

You are welcome, *Penthouse Forum.*

As it turned out, amazingly, I was not living completely in a
fantasy. Fernando, unaware of all the pentagrams I had drawn to
summon his lust, *was* attracted to me, which I learned one spring
night a few years later when he kissed me in his parents' bedroom.
The kiss lasted for about five seconds—just long enough for me to
think, *Holy shit, we are kissing,* and then awkwardly dart my
tongue into his mouth as though I were stamping a time card.
Then Fernando drew back, looked into my eyes, and said: "This
doesn't mean anything. And you can never tell anyone." Obviously it meant everything and I told everyone. But more on that
later.

Second Base: ?

I *think* Fernando *maybe* touched my right boob during our life-
changing five-second make-out. But it's also possible I skipped
second base entirely and went straight to . . .

Home Base: Age Twenty

Yup, you read that right. I stole *two* bases just so I could lose my
virginity before I graduated from college. In fact, my next book
could be a helpful intimacy guide for nuns and people who've
spent roughly ages twelve to thirty-five in solitary confinement or
a coma. I think I'll call it *Just Do It: From Kissing to Intercourse in
Four Short Years.* I don't think Nike will mind.

Third Base: Age Twenty-One

Because you should only put your mouth on the genitalia of people you actually like. If there's one quote from this book I want meaningfully tattooed on people's forearms, that's it.

⌒

But backing up for a moment . . . After Fernando's painful rejection, I didn't touch another boy for the rest of high school—not that I had many opportunities. I still didn't get invited to parties and spent my senior year infatuated with a classmate who would later turn out to be gay. Anna, meanwhile, began an intense phone relationship with an older guy based on his belief that she was someone else. It was pretty much par for our course.

I didn't fare much better when I got to college. In fact, it got worse. Because instead of owning up to my inexperience, I decided to lie about it.

Before you judge me, two things you should know:

1. My freshman year roommate, Carolyn, was the most beautiful woman I had ever seen in real life. A genetically blessed mix of French, English, and Vietnamese, she looked like a young Christy Turlington with a Euro-chic wardrobe and edgy asymmetrical bob. Instantly she was the most sought-after person on campus, and I became known far and wide as "Carolyn's Roommate."

2. I don't know if it's still like this, or if I just happened to be placed into a dorm of oversharing nymphomaniacs, but at Wesleyan University in 1998, asking a person how many blow jobs she'd given was considered an acceptable social icebreaker. By the second day of college, we were pretty much sitting around dictating our sexual histories to each other while chain-smoking—an experience that

at the time went for about thirty-two thousand dollars a year.

I could have just told them I was a virgin. It wasn't like it would have been shocking, based on my acne and tendency to wear bulbous-toed platform sneakers that looked to have been cobbled by cartoon elves. But I saw the opportunity to reinvent myself—to rewrite history according to the unrealized fantasies of my youth—and I jumped at it. I told everyone that I had an on-again, off-again boyfriend back home, who had taken my innocence over the summer, in between acting jobs. He was sexy and a little bit mean, keeping me on the hook while he gallivanted around with C-list movie stars—even though I was the one he truly loved, a confession he would whisper in my ear after one of our vigorous yet tender lovemaking sessions. His name, of course, was Fernando.

~~Sex~~ Six Good Reasons Not to Lie About Losing Your Virginity, from Someone Who Knows

1. It is wrong.

I'm not going to tell you you should never lie, because I lie a lot. Some lies, like pretending to be sick so you don't have to put pants on and go see a friend's improv show, are fairly harmless. Others, like inventing major life experiences, sexual escapades, or professional credentials, are not. In some cases, you may actually be breaking a law.

2. It is nuts.

It may come from a place of insecurity, but it is still insane in a non-charming way to pretend that someone—especially someone who actually exists and whose name you don't even bother to change (see next list)—has ravished your body and made you a wo/man.

3. You have to pretend to know things you don't know.

Picture that scene from *The 40-Year-Old Virgin* when Steve Carell is describing touching a woman's breasts and how they feel like bags of sand and you get the idea.

4. You might develop an undeserved reputation.

With my newfound freedom to bend the truth, I became a sexual legend in my own mind and, apparently, in the minds of others. In fact, at the start of my junior year, I—still a virgin!—was listed on the men's bathroom wall as Best Fuck on Campus. As it turns out, you can get around without actually getting around, and become a slut before you have ever even seen a penis in person.

5. When you lose your virginity for real, there is no one to tell.

The absolute best and most important reason not to lie about losing your virginity is so that you can tell the person you actually lose it to that he or she is your first. I was lucky enough to lose mine, at age twenty and three-quarters, to a very nice boy who liked me a lot, and it didn't hurt or make me bleed or any of the other things I worried about that might "give me away," but it still makes me profoundly sad to know that I kept up a stupid, pointless lie instead of making myself vulnerable at a moment when it really would have been worth it to let my guard down. Perhaps because of the resulting self-loathing, I broke things off with that boy shortly after the deed was done. And I wish I could say I never lied about it again, but . . .

6. You have to keep the lie going forever.

You can't just turn around and say to your friends, "Hey, guys, remember that extensive backstory I told you about Fernando and all the sexy sex positions we did? None of that actually happened. Ha-ha." They will back away slowly and never speak to you again.

You can start telling the real story to any new friends you make, but you have to keep a detailed list of who believes the lie so that you don't inadvertently reveal your deep mental issues to the people who know you best.

And One Very Good Reason Not to Make the Fake Virginity-Taker a Real Person, If You Insist on Lying

1. If you are dumb enough to name a *real, live* person in your elaborate lie, chances are one hundred percent that at some point later in life, that real person will end up in the same room with someone you lied to about all the sex you had with him, and you will have to run interference as your trusting friend makes confusing small talk with your oblivious pretend penetrator. (The only situation slightly more awkward is if you lie about someone dying and then that person appears at a cocktail party, so please make sure to fake only the deaths of the already deceased. Pro tip from me to you.)

The upside to all of this is that I did finally lose my virginity and have continued to have non-lie-based sex for the past decade and a half, primarily with my husband, who might be the only person on earth who has always known both the real and the fake stories of my deflowerment. However, in return for his nonjudgmental devotion, he did make me promise not to write about our sex life in this book. I said I wouldn't, and, as you all know, I would never lie.

Just this one thing:

Seven Things No One Tells You About Postbaby Sex

1. Babies are the world's biggest cockblock.

Ironic, I know, considering how they got here. But the first few times Jeff and I attempted to rekindle the romance, our son—perhaps sensing the potential biological threat of additional offspring—refused to cooperate. Time after time, we attempted to put him down in his bassinet, only to hear him squeal moments later as we prepared to doff our spit-up-stained sweatpants. Once we finally succeeded, it was a hurried affair, and not as enjoyable for me as I would have liked—not because of any failure on the part of my husband, but because it was impossible for me not to worry that my equipment had been . . . well, compromised.

2. You will have an identity crisis between your thighs.

Once you've pushed a baby through an orifice you once reserved for recreational purposes, it's hard to go back, psychologically speaking. That's not always a bad thing—I recently needed encouragement to finish a stressful project on deadline, and a friend put her hand on mine and told me, with some very meaningful eye contact, "You gave birth. You can do *anything*"—but when you're in the throes of passion and suddenly you find yourself thinking, *A head came out of there!*, it kind of puts a damper on the proceedings. I remember my tenth-grade health teacher, Ms. Drvostep, gravely informing the class during a discussion of human sexuality that, at least biologically, the anus was designed as an "out hole." Maybe that's the problem. My vagina was an in hole, then it was (briefly, but memorably) an out hole, and now it's supposed to be an in hole again. It's having an identity crisis, and it doesn't help that sometimes, when I'm drying off after a shower, Jeff will point at my crotch and exclaim gleefully to Sam, "There's your old house!"

3. It's hard not to picture your vagina as one of those wind socks you see at the airport, for the rest of time.

There is also the uncomfortable (double entendre intended) truth that it's hard to go back, physiologically speaking, even if your doctor gives you the go-ahead after six weeks, which is the standard abstinence period gratefully celebrated by the new mom and ascetically endured by the new dad (the wait time is even longer following a cesarean section). No matter how many Kegels you do, the fact remains that a fully formed human being weighing around eight pounds came out of an opening previously accustomed to visitors of a smaller girth. An old Lenny Bruce routine once compared a large penis to a baby's arm, but add a second arm, two legs, a torso, and a head that feels, from the inside, like a bowling ball set on fire, and you have something not at all like a penis. So naturally there is going to be some fallout (no pun intended! none!) from the stretching. No one wants to talk about it, of course. I mean, I'm always seeing tabloid covers crowing about some celebrity or other's fabulous postbaby body, which she presumably has achieved through a combination of colonic therapy, macrobiotic diet, and virgin sacrifice. But I never see an article about, say, Jessica Alba's postbaby vagina. And if hers isn't ready for the pages of *Us Weekly*, then what hope is there for the rest of us?

4. Bon Jovi's *Slippery When Wet* is just taunting you now.

Postbaby sex is a slippery slope even under the best of circumstances, and I'm not speaking literally, as anyone who's experienced the drying effects of plummeting postpartum estrogen can attest.

5. Better get used to the term "MILF," because that is all you are allowed to be now (if anyone wants to have sex with you at all).

Even if you do get over the libido-robbing hormone fiesta and the colicky coitus interruptus and manage to retain enviable nether-regional muscle tone and semiregular bedpost notching, there's one thing that no amount of personal grooming or mood music can change, and that's the realization that you're now somebody's mother. As such, society now gives you two exciting choices, a special procreative variation on the traditional Madonna/whore:

either succumb to the high-waisted jeans, sensible earlobe-length haircut, and soccer-friendly SUV of the asexual martyr who lives in a Tide commercial, or get a gym membership, hop on the treadmill, and run like hell for MILF Island.

The term "MILF" itself might be the problem. I've always disliked it, and not just because it's icky and sophomoric, but because it suggests that a mother who's considered sexually desirable is an endangered species on a par with the Tasmanian devil or the giant panda. I like to think I am at least as sexy as a regular-size panda on days I've managed to shower.

6. Sex toys become literal.

Get ready to roll over in the heat of passion and find Mr. Potato Head's nose trying to force its way into your butt. Not as kinky as it sounds.

7. Just kidding. It's actually pretty awesome.

Despite all the awkwardness and body dysmorphia I've mentioned, I'm happy to report that I still very much enjoy sex when conditions are ideal (baby, asleep; me, awake) and that, despite what my sense memory occasionally tells me, no part of my anatomy resembles the Holland Tunnel, even in passing. Postbaby sex can even feel sometimes like the carefree sex of my youth, except that it's faster and more exhausted—not to be confused with exhaustive—and we can't make any noise. And we never even consider not using protection in the heat of the moment, because, I mean, seriously, look where that got us.

To be extra cautious, we should probably just stick to the stuff *real* fantasies are made of: getting drunk, stuffing our faces with bar snacks, and talking about all the other people we wish we could have sex with.

ANSWERS I WOULD LIKE TO CHANGE
IN RETROSPECT

Year: 1983

Context: Naked, examining the posterior of my best friend, Salvador

Question: What are you playing, Una?

What I Wish I'd Said: Doctor

What I Actually Said: Look in butt!

Year: 1991

Context: The PS 282 Fifth Grade Sudden-Death Geography Bee, in front of my entire class

Question: On which island is Hawaii's capital located: Maui or Oahu?

What I Wish I'd Said: Oahu

What I Actually Said: Maui

Year: 1998

Context: My mom treating me to a pricey haircut during fall break from my first semester of college

Question: What if we went *short* short, like Mia Farrow's in *Rosemary's Baby*?

What I Wish I'd Said: No, thanks, I'm pretty sure I'd look more like 1980s-era Billy Crystal with adult acne.

What I Actually Said: Okay.

Year: 2006

Context: Upon returning home after a drunken dinner party, my boyfriend, Jeff, dropping to his knees in our apartment vestibule

Question: Marry me?

What I Wish I'd Said: Yes, yes, a hundred times yes!
What I Actually Said: Fuck you.

Year: 2012
Context: Cocktail hour following a friend's nuptials
Question: Would you like to try a mini Reuben?
What I Wish I'd Said: Yes, yes, a *million* times yes!
What I Actually Said: No.

Rules for Sitcom Living

Most people do not know this, but from late 2003 through mid-2005 I was part of the cast of *Friends*.

Some of you may be thinking, *But* Friends *ended in May 2004, Una*. To which I say, touché. You have a keen eye. I was not actually on the show *Friends*. But I was one of three twentysomething women living in close proximity to three twentysomething men, and it was the mid-aughts, and so for those eighteen months you could not attempt to microwave a frozen burrito without someone trying to claim that *they* were the Chandler of the group.

To be sure, there were some details separating the six of us from NBC's all-star ensemble. For example, my roommates, Betsy and Ellaree, and I did not live in a sprawling, eclectically chic Manhattan apartment but rather on the third floor of a charmless row house in Brooklyn with thin walls and carpeting the color of eggnog someone had ashed in at the office Christmas party. Our male counterparts, Kabir, Bajir, and Alex, lived in a similarly unimpressive (and much filthier) pad fifteen minutes away, but we treated their apartment like it was right across the hall, often showing up still in our pajama pants. *Kabir, Bajir, and Alex* sounds more like its own spin-off show about two Muslim grad students forced to room with a pretty, neurotic tomboy—or maybe a feisty

Labrador—but actually they were three tall, strapping white guys, two of whom happened to grow up together in a Sufi fellowship in Pennsylvania and one of whom wore Al Franken glasses and collected superhero figurines.

Everyone knows that there are rules that come with living in a sitcom, and we tried our best to adhere to the clichés. We had the "guy's girl" in Ellaree, a stunningly gorgeous but socially awkward comic geek; and the "girl's guy" in Kabir, a lush-lipped sensitive singer-songwriter and elementary school teacher who set Rumi poems to acoustic guitar music in his free time. Bajir was the kooky artist, Betsy the mother hen, Alex the nebbishy brain. I was the one who accidentally bleach-stained all the towels with her benzoyl-peroxide-laden acne masks and who kept everyone up to date on *The Bachelorette*. (So, basically the Chandler.)

Group friendships can be tricky. I spent my senior year of college living with four other women, and while I still love them dearly, our house was a minefield of perceived slights, long-held grudges, and carefully plotted emotional manipulations. We spent that year playing an off-screen game of *Survivor*—forging and breaking alliances, voting people out of the house during tense family meetings, and sustaining ourselves with strange, desperate food choices, like pad thai made with reduced-fat Skippy peanut butter and baby carrots.

But somehow, living with Bergen-Butler (as we came to call ourselves, based on the names of our streets) was easy. Our personalities meshed in a magical way that almost never happens outside of romantic comedies. Sure, we had moments of conflict— there was that time when Ellaree went on vacation and sublet her room via craigslist to someone who turned out to be a wanted criminal and the incident in which Bajir secretly rubbed one of Alex's tea bags on his balls and then replaced it in the jar—but for the most part we were a cast of characters with enviably natural chemistry.

I think the fact that we were co-ed helped us a lot. At the risk of making broad generalizations across gender lines—get ready!—women and men tend to approach friendships . . . differently. Women, in my experience, assess potential friends based on a wide variety of factors, including but not limited to emotional intelligence, sense of humor, vocabulary, aerobic activity level, last-minute plan cancellation percentage, number of shared enemies, rate of mood swings, and DVR queue (both length and content). Men, on the other hand, when meeting someone new, pretty much just need the other person not to punch them in the face right away and they are instant BFFs.

In high school, my friend Anna and I once came up with a math equation for deciding whether we should be friends with a given person.

"If someone sucks more than twenty-five percent of the time," Anna said, "then that is not cool, and we should not be friends with them."

"Unless," I countered, "they suck so much that it becomes kind of fun to witness them sucking so hard."

"Agreed," Anna said.

We went back to our anagrams.

So, the Una and Anna Friend Assessment Chart reflects the priorities of human beings and other highly intelligent animals/machines who are at least a little bit petty and mean.

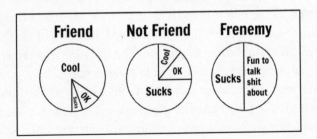

The Male Friend Assessment Chart, I suspect, has much less guile.

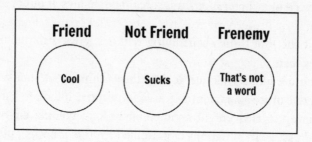

I learned this firsthand when I lived full-time with Kabir, Bajir, and Alex one summer when I needed a place to crash, before I moved in with Betsy and Ellaree. Rooming with boys was incredibly refreshing psychologically and unbelievably unrefreshing physically. There were never any passive-aggressive power plays, and yet there were also never any towels or dishes that didn't smell at least a little bit like ass. Kabir once made a huge pot of chili, accidentally substituting a half cup of cayenne pepper for the half cup of paprika the recipe called for. The result—totally inedible, even by the boys' low standards—sat on the stove for weeks, growing mold, until they finally just duct-taped the lid shut and left it on the curb outside.

But aside from the smells, my exile in Guyville was some of the most fun I've ever had. The boys enforced a set of whimsical house rules that made little to no sense, like "anyone can force another roommate to do ten push-ups at any time" and "if one roommate takes his shirt off, everyone has to."* Alex, a film major, had rigged a NASA-level sound system for his DVD player, and so most nights we ordered in Thai food and bonded over our

*This one, possibly, was invented just so they could see my boobs. I will never know.

shared love of high culture. I introduced the boys to *Sex and the City*; they showed me *Debbie Does Dallas*. Ironically and unexpectedly freed of self-consciousness, I happily ate myself out of all my pants.

But the best thing about living with the guys was the "Stairway" Clean.

The deceptively simple goal of the "Stairway" Clean was to clean the entire apartment in the eight minutes it took to listen to "Stairway to Heaven" at a ridiculously loud volume on Bajir's record player. In situations of extreme filth (i.e., *always*), playing the song multiple times was allowed, although a two- or three-"Stairway" Clean was considered a failure.

Of course, one of the cardinal rules of the sitcom is that when a group of people cohabitate, assuming they are over eighteen and not related, romance and/or sexual tension must ensue. I need to pause here to make a quick appeal to television writers and show runners across the globe: *Please* please please please please if you are doing a will-they-or-won't-they story arc with two lead characters, *do not* let them hook up until the series finale. The buildup is deliciously intoxicating and sometimes actually makes me squee out loud, but then once they get together, after an initial surge of elation there is a long, boring plateau of *meh*. It's kind of like having a few years of foreplay with your most lusted-after crush, finally getting laid, and then having him continue to hump your leg for five more seasons as you lie there, slowly developing a urinary tract infection.

I would say that we wisely made the decision not to get involved with one another on a genital-to-genital level, but I think it wasn't so much a "decision" in retrospect as it was a collective "complete lack of ability to effectively hit on *anyone*, let alone a close friend." We all fell in love with one another, but we tended to express that love in pajama-clad cuddling and bummed cigarettes or, if we were feeling bold, meaningful Beatles songs strummed ineptly on Kabir's guitar. One lonely weekend when Alex and I were the only ones in town, we engaged in a brief, awkward dalliance, but within days we were back to being platonic friends again, as if the Bergen-Butler group dynamic was so powerful that it could absorb and eradicate any emotional fallout from ill-advised sex acts between its members. Now *that's* what I call friends with benefits.

THE "STAIRWAY" CLEAN:
A STEP-BY-STEP GUIDE TO ACHIEVING
ROBERT PLANT–LEVEL CLEANLINESS

1. Put on "Stairway to Heaven" at the loudest volume you can tolerate (should be able to drown out vacuuming, stress weeping).

2. Begin slowly, in keeping with the Renaissance Faire-y recorder intro. Pick up stray socks, underpants, and desiccated french fries from the carpet as if gathering wildflowers in a serene meadow.

3. During the first chorus, make your bed—but don't fold any corners. Drape decorative shawl over desk clutter; throw errant objects into closet or nearest trash can.

4. During the fifteen seconds of instrumental music before Robert Plant first croons "Ooooooh, it makes me wonder," sprint through the house holding a feather duster outstretched in each hand.

5. Use second and third choruses to drown bathroom in as much Scrubbing Bubbles as you can pour with one hand while simultaneously plunging toilet.

6. Stop for a high-five with your co–"Stairway" Cleaners (if applicable) at the halfway mark, and remove shirt, per house rules or just because you are filthy. (Shirt now becomes acceptable rag for all-purpose cleaning.)

7. During fourth and fifth choruses, vacuum all carpeted surfaces or strap scrub brushes to feet and pretend you are Apolo Ohno (tip: watch out for pets and electrical cords).

8. The guitar solo around six and a half minutes in is your cue to attack the kitchen with a head-banging vengeance. Wash dishes, throwing away any that are too grime-encrusted to be cleaned in five seconds.

9. As Plant wails the final chorus, wipe down kitchen sur-

faces and tie trash bags, shoving them into a mudroom or hallway if possible.

10. Shriek in panic as music begins to slow down; throw any remaining mess into closets, purses, or fridge. Liberally spray Febreze.

11. By the time Plant sings the last line, collapse on the couch in a sweaty heap.

12. Repeat every month until smell becomes overpowering and you have to move.

Achilles' Wheel

How I Learned to Drive

There are a lot of things the members of my family aren't known for, like being able to throw a Frisbee reliably, using an at-home waxing kit successfully, or agreeing to go on a hike without first making a lot of attempts to get out of it. But if I had to pick just one thing at which we overwhelmingly fail as a team it would probably be driving.

My mother didn't learn to drive until she was thirty-eight. This, combined with the sort of overly cautious nature that leads her to arrive at airports three hours early, has resulted in an anxious road temperament. Every car, mammal, and stationary object that enters her peripheral vision has the effect of a hideous jack-in-the-box. She will literally gasp when another car approaches to merge into her beloved far-right lane, even if the driver has a yield sign. She brakes for *everything*.

On the other side of the genetic pool is my dad, who drives in a manner that suggests a deeply ingrained death wish. This started in 1970, when my then-sixteen-year-old father, behind the wheel of an especially choice 1964 Rambler American, rear-ended another car in the middle of the Gold Star Memorial Bridge in Connecticut. At the time, he was wearing a pair of star-spangled overalls that he liked to unfasten while driving due to the fact that they were (in keeping with the style of the times) uncomfortably snug in the crotch. As he stepped out of the car to assess the damage, the overalls fell to the ground . . . which doesn't say anything about his driving, really, but which is integral to the telling of this story at cocktail parties. He is an easily distractible driver, prone to looking over his shoulder to make direct eye contact with backseat passengers or swerving between lanes while attempting to answer a seemingly endless stream of hands-free phone calls, though on paper he has a surprisingly clean record.*

⌒

Like every American child of the eighties raised on *Knight Rider* and Billy Ocean, I have an entire album's worth of photos of myself posing behind the wheel of various cars, trying to look cool. I don't look cool, at all, in any of them. Maybe it's the unibrow, maybe it's the corduroy jumpsuits, or maybe it's because my parents seemed drawn to the types of jalopies you usually see balanced on concrete blocks in abandoned junkyards. When we lived in suburban Texas we had a cute, reasonably clean baby blue Volkswagen Rabbit, but when we moved back to New York in 1988 it got hit on the street while parked and my parents traded it in for a used 1979 Datsun 210 the color of a jaundiced polar bear.

When we brought the Datsun home, there were jugs of gasoline rolling around in the food-stained trunk. This was during a period when car radio theft was rampant in New York; you'd often see parked cars with their front window smashed in and the cassette desk missing from the dashboard. Lots of people made hand-lettered signs to warn off would-be thieves, promising that there was no radio to steal, but our Datsun didn't need one. "I bet

---

*His worst offense? Introducing an eight-year-old to the word "cockmaster" during a burst of road rage. That or the star-spangled overalls; it's kind of a toss-up.

I could leave the key in the ignition with the engine running and it would still be here in the morning," my dad would brag to our neighbors, patting one of the ripped, pus-colored imitation leather seats with pride while my sister and I gulped fresh air through cracks in the windows.

Since we lived in brownstone Brooklyn, around the corner from a major subway station, we hardly ever actually needed the car to go anywhere. Mostly it was used for quick trips across the street a few times a week to avoid being ticketed. (New York City gets its trademark sparkling cleanliness from street sweepers that patrol the streets every other day at the crack of dawn, shoving used condoms, abandoned hair weaves, and dead squirrels into the gutters while urban car owners idle, double-parked, cursing loudly in their pajamas.) Even when we did take the rare road trip to visit relatives in New England, I never paid attention to the mechanics of driving, since I was too busy singing Madonna's entire *Immaculate Collection* at top volume. Thieves might be able to steal our radio, but they would never take my passionate rendition of "La Isla Bonita" away.

By the time I turned sixteen, when most kids my age were lining up to get their learner's permits, the Datsun had finally been jettisoned after failing to pass a routine inspection. There was no driver's ed at my high school, and no one I knew seemed to care all that much about acquiring what was, at least within the city limits, a nonessential skill. So I focused my energies on loftier pursuits like studying for the SATs, clipping eye makeup tutorials out of *Cosmopolitan*, and amassing a soon-to-be obsolete VHS archive of every single episode of *Melrose Place*. Two years later, when I turned eighteen, my father personally escorted me to the local Board of Elections so that I could register to vote. Some things were important according to our family ethos, and some weren't. The latter category, based on generations of athletic underachievement, included pretty much any physical skill that wasn't automatically taken care of by the central nervous system. In related news, I still cannot whistle, snap my fingers, or do a cartwheel. But hey, at least I got to cast an absentee ballot for Al Gore.

⌒

If the movie *Clueless* had never been written, I might never have learned how to drive. You know how sometimes you look back at your life and you realize with awe and wonder that hundreds of tiny, fated details had to line up just so for you to be where you are today? Well, if I hadn't fallen down the stone steps of the outdoor amphitheater during my group tour of Swarthmore College and been forced to attend Wesleyan University for shame avoidance purposes,* and if Wesleyan hadn't then randomly placed me in the dorm room directly above a sassy gay boy from Georgia named Charlie Meyer, and if we both hadn't had the same unironic appreciation for Alicia Silverstone, and if he hadn't gotten me drunk on Southern Comfort and made me confess my stunning lack of sexual exploits up to that point, this essay might not even exist. But as it was, all those things came to be, and that is how Charlie Meyer took to tormenting me with the bitchy zinger "You're a virgin who can't drive." (Don't worry, I got him back eventually, by projectile vomiting vodka-spiked Kool-Aid into the backseat of his prized Toyota Land Cruiser.) Anyway, it took four years of college and then another three of sheepishly handing my passport to smirking bartenders, but eventually I got tired of the jokes and decided it was time for me to literally and figuratively take the wheel.

I finally got out of my dreams and into a car (well, not *my* car, but I'm sure Mr. Ocean will understand) when I was twenty-five

---

*And also because I was rejected from Swarthmore. One more place I can never go back (see page 50).

years old and suffering/slothing my way through a six-month bout of unemployment.

I'd signed up for driving school on the Internet, precharging my credit card for ten lessons so that I couldn't wuss out. This kind of online shopping roulette can backfire, as when I designed a personalized crystal whiskey decanter from Pottery Barn after drunkenly watching an entire season of *Mad Men* on Netflix and played chicken with the order button (it is now a very expensive, monogrammed piggy bank). But a trunkful of crocheted shortalls from Anthropologie can't honk outside your apartment for fifteen minutes, and so I was forced to follow through when the frigid February morning of my vehicular baptism arrived.

I aced the SATs, I reminded myself as I stumbled downstairs on shaking legs for my first lesson, my heart threatening to stall inside my chest. *I was Fidel Castro in my high school's mock UN, and I convinced Jesus to strip human rights away from dissenters. I made Phi Beta Kappa! I can fucking drive a fucking car.* I ignored the fact that these were all intellectual achievements—which had nothing to do with the large motor skills or directional acuity that were conspicuously absent from my DNA. I felt sure that if I talked the talk, I could maneuver a huge hunk of metal and rubber through morning rush hour city traffic. At least without killing anyone. Probably.

My instructor's name was Mr. Council. He was exactly how his name makes him sound: judicial, instructional, taciturn. Since he was a middle-aged, world-weary-looking black man and I was a young, eager, and inept white girl, I thought there might be buddy-comedy potential for us, but he was not amused by me. That became clear from the very first moment, when I got into the car and attempted to pull out into traffic without taking the gearshift out of park. He sighed heavily. I would come to know this as his primary form of communication.

Mr. Council sighed when I nervously abused the clutch, inching toward stop signs as if I were using the tire screeches to send messages in Morse code. He sighed when I clicked the wrong turn signal or accidentally turned on the windshield wipers. Sometimes he would trade the sighing for a long, annoyed stare, which I would get when I lost control of my inner monologue and began to frantically narrate my every thought. ("Aaaah! Sorry, I should have pulled out farther for that left! Ha-ha! . . . That trucker is honking at me! Is that, like, road flirting or is he mad because I cut him off? . . . Okay, now I'm putting on my signal to park. . . . Oops, reverse! Aaand I almost hit that biker. But I didn't! Phew. Wait, how did I just pop the hood? Is this *not* the air-conditioning?") He used his passenger-side brake liberally and liked to give me deadpan criticism without looking up from his newspaper.

"So what were you just practicing?" he would ask as we sat in a dead-end lot in Red Hook.

"A three-point turn," I replied in my best teacher's pet voice. "Also known as a K-turn or a broken U-turn. Or, in Ireland—"

"And how many points did you just hit?"

"I don't know exactly. I got confused by the backward lettering of that No Trespassing sign in the rearview."

"Take a guess."

"Um . . . nine?"

"And what do you call that?"

". . . A nine-point turn?"

He slammed down his paper. "A failed driving test. Do it again."

My fellow New York drivers were not particularly sensitive to my plight. Although I was driving a vehicle marked *clearly* and one might even say *humiliatingly* on all sides with the words "Student Driver," people saw no reason to let me take my time. Halfway through my first lesson, a burly man leaned out his window to tell me, "Learn how to drive!"

"I *am*!" I yelled back.

Mr. Council sighed.

Soon, despite the eight hundred dollars burning a hole in my credit score, I started skipping lessons out of pure cowardice. I hated learning to drive, mostly because I was not immediately good at it and also because parallel parking had replaced my previous, long-held greatest fear of a rat swimming up through our toilet. And so, when eight o'clock on Tuesday rolled around one especially self-esteem-challenging week, I buried myself under the covers and pretended not to hear the beeping outside. My boyfriend, getting dressed for work, peered out the window.

"Isn't that your car?" he asked. I poked my head out of my tent of shame.

"Uh, it shouldn't be," I mumbled. "I canceled."

"Well, he's definitely out there waiting," Jeff said.

"I don't know why, because I *called and canceled.*" I was unreasonably indignant in the way that only a liar can be. I did not call and cancel. I woke up feeling terrified, knowing that each driving lesson was an exercise in failure that would inevitably lead to the truly horrifying experience of failing my road test.

On good days I reminded myself that any idiot could drive, but on bad days I began to convince myself I was the only idiot who couldn't. After all, I could never do the bumper cars as a kid. I was the one the amusement park guy had to ride with and steer for. I couldn't even *crash* correctly. And so I hid week after week under the sheets until Mr. Council and his dreaded second brake gave up on me. In the spring, my unemployment ended, and having a job gave me a great excuse to actually cancel my lessons. I threw myself into my work and took time each day to relish my relative proficiency in skills like walking upright and swiping my Metro-Card at subway turnstiles. I still cringed when forced to present my learner's permit to bouncers, but consoled myself by developing a theory that maybe I was just not *meant* to drive, just like some people are gay and some people like Enya.

What finally pushed me over the edge was my nineteen-year-old sister's proclamation that October that *she* was going to get her license. There were three things that, as the slightly more competitive but considerably less brave sister, I had always promised myself I'd do before Zoe did: (1) graduate from college; (2) lose my virginity; and (3) drive a car. Even though I'm six years older I barely beat her to sex, and I wasn't willing to let another rite of passage—that was rightfully mine to screw up first!—bite the dust.

I still had a few lesson credits left, so I stuck with the driving school but requested a new instructor, who turned out to be someone named Mr. Lester. He looked like a septuagenarian cross between Dean Martin and Humphrey Bogart, except he wore sweater vests and a toupee. Unlike Mr. Council, Mr. Lester was kind and corny and avuncular and I instantly liked him, which assuaged my fear enough for me to actually learn a few things. Over the course of our four lessons together, Mr. Lester successfully taught me how to parallel park using formulas and angles, a vast improvement over the "fingers crossed!" approach I had been using. He taught me to peer over the wheel as I advanced after stop signs, looking frantically right and left, prepared to slam on the brakes should anything move. While I practiced, he told me inspirational stories about teaching his oldest student, a seventy-year-old woman, how to drive. I liked the stories until they ended with her passing her road test and I was reminded that when it came to driving even my grandma could handily kick my ass.

After our last lesson before my road test, Mr. Lester dropped me off with a cheery farewell. He wouldn't be working the next day, when my road test was scheduled, so another instructor would be chaperoning me in a new and unfamiliar Student Driver car.

"I think you've got a pretty good chance," he said, sticking his arm out the window to shoot me an enthusiastic thumbs-up. "Just remember to put the car in drive before you step on the gas, okay? Otherwise they'll fail you right there at the curb."

As I watched Mr. Lester drive away I got the feeling in the pit of my stomach I used to get when my parents dropped me off at nursery school. There were no longer any obstacles standing between me and the open road . . . except, of course, for whatever imminent, stupendous disgrace the fates had in store. Would I forget to signal? Make my trademark nine-point turn? Hit a mailman? That night, I dreamed that I was driving an out-of-control car through a forest, topless.

I managed to put clothes on for my test, but in keeping with my nightmare scenario, the DMV examiner I was assigned to the next morning was a gnarled old man with a limp so severe that his left foot was turned perpendicular to his body, forcing him to use a misshapen cane that looked to have been home-whittled. As he approached the car I wondered if I should get out and help him. I finally decided not to offer a hand to the handicapped arbiter of my transportational future, just in case he took offense and failed me for not understanding power lock doors. He grunted a little as he eased slowly into the passenger seat, but then the stress melted from his face and he offered me a faint smile.

"Relax," he said. "This will be over before you know it."

The actual test, the thing I had been dreading for almost a decade of my adult life, was surprisingly easy at first. I pulled out and inched down the street, doing a cool fifteen miles per hour. I stopped at a stop sign. At the examiner's request, I made a right turn. And then . . .

"Parallel park behind that car." I pulled up next to a blue sedan, my pulse racing. I checked my blind spot and put the car in reverse. I grasped for a psychological moment of Zen, but all I could summon was the smarmy face of the late Corey Haim on the *License to Drive* poster. I began to reverse, but immediately all my memorized formulas flew out the window, and I guessed at a forty-five-degree angle, then locked the wheel left. We slowly rolled into the space.

"Good," the examiner said matter-of-factly. "Pull out." He asked me to make a left turn, and then another, and another, until we were back on the street where we started. He told me to pull over and park. And then he told me that I passed.

I had expected a wave of elation, but instead I felt the same kind of underwhelmed surprise as I had when I'd lost my virginity: Oh. That was *it*? It makes sense in retrospect; angels blowing trumpets are probably in short supply and only get booked for extraordinary achievements, like when you saw off your own trapped foot with a beer opener and still manage to climb out of a deep, treacherous ravine. Things like sex and driving seem like huge milestones on approach, but once you get there, you realize that pretty much every other person on earth, regardless of IQ or fitness level, has crossed the finish line ahead of you, and that you are just one more idiot who has managed to hoist herself over one of humanity's lower bars.

Still, eight years later, I continue to present my legitimate license to bouncers and TSA workers, filled with pride that I am legally allowed to operate a motor vehicle within the contiguous (and noncontiguous!) United States, despite being prone to driving with the parking brake engaged, reversing by accident, and leaving the high beams on overnight.

I'll see *you* on the road.

Shopping for Godot

Sometimes it feels like I've spent my entire life searching for that elusive something that will finally make me truly happy. I've looked everywhere: J.Crew, the Sharper Image, IKEA . . . even in the weird Vermont Country Store catalog I get every Christmas that somehow sells both fruitcakes and dildos. But I still haven't found that holy grail of modern capitalist lust: the one product that will forever make me whole. I know it's out there somewhere and that I *must* possess it. In this way it's kind of like Frodo's ring, and I am Gollum, only with pastier skin and less patience.

In 1986, I thought I had found it in the She-Ra Princess of Power Crystal Castle, and for weeks I took to strutting around my house the way I figure people like Mark Zuckerberg and Willow Smith—people who've struck gold early in life—must walk everywhere they go, thinking, *I've got it made. From here on out, it's nothing but frosted Pop-Tarts and world domination.* Alas, my ennui returned shortly thereafter, and I sold my She-Ra castle at a yard sale for eight dollars.

Year after year, the story has always been the same: covet, obtain, discard. I never had a favorite toy because there was always something new on the horizon, and the ones I'd grown tired of sat unplayed with on a shelf like a bored, plastic harem.

In retrospect this behavior probably predicted my credit card abuse as an adult. Sometimes, as I'm drifting off to sleep, I imagine conversations—and maybe even entire training seminars—about me that are happening at the American Express headquarters:

Specialist #1: Hey, do you have a minute? I'm worried about Una.

Specialist #2: Why, did she buy another set of silk gaucho pants from Anthropologie on fire sale?

Specialist #1: No . . . but she paid her bill on March 16, for a total of $987.54, and as of yesterday she's only re-spent $614.03.

Specialist #2: Oh, my God. It's been three days and she hasn't maxed out yet?

Specialist #1: I know, right? That's not like her.

Specialist #2: Do you think she died?

Specialist #1: Oh, man, she *did* just buy a stud finder.

Specialist #2: Nah, I don't think those are sharp, and also, I'm pretty sure that charge was a porn site.

Specialist #1: I'm still worried.

Specialist #2: Okay. Send her an e-mail offer for twenty dollars off the entire set of Mattel *Beverly Hills, 90210* dolls and if she doesn't place an order within the hour, I'll make an anonymous 911 call.

Yes, I have a little bit of a problem. Some call it consumerism, some call it greed, some call it hoarding. I call it hope, with interest.

A BRIEF CHRONOLOGY OF CONSPICUOUS
CONSUMPTION

~

Part I, 1980s

Dawn of the Dolls

~

My favorite heroine of literature is Eloise, that precocious, eter-
nally messy-haired six-year-old convinced that her borderline-
psychotic inner fantasy life is interesting enough to carry an
entire series.

If forced to choose, I think my favorite thing about Eloise is her
devotion to her dolls: Saylor, a wide-eyed baby with no arms, and
Sabine, a Jamaican rag doll. While I, like Eloise, am a city child, I
could never identify with her whimsically negligent Upper East
Side upbringing. I didn't have an elevator building or a private
tutor or a British nanny, and in order to qualify for room service
at my house, you either had to
spike a fever or vomit uncontrollably, which tended to take away
from its luxury. But doll obsession?
Now, *that* was my jam.

My parents leaned hippie, so my
dolls didn't get good until I learned
how to talk, and, more specifically,
to say, *Please stop making me sleep
with the creepy sandpaper voodoo
phallus some friend of yours brought
back from Chile and get me a Pound
Puppy.*

Eventually, I did get a Pound
Puppy, whom I named Harold. I

*His name was Mr. Chile,
because I was creative.*

also had a Cabbage Patch doll named Ethel. All my dolls, for some reason, received good, solid, farmhand-sounding names that had been out of popular use since the 1940s. My friend Abby, on the other hand, pulled off what I consider the PR move of a lifetime when she named a cheap and generic bald baby doll Fancy. The name instantly gave Fancy—who, if memory serves, could generally be found floating naked in a puddle out by Abby's dad's metalwork shed—a sort of European allure. Maybe she was facedown because she drank watered-down table wine, like French children. Maybe her nudity was an exotic life choice.

By 1984, my tastes had matured enough that I set my sights on the Cadillac of dolls, Barbie. Unfortunately, I was in no way qualified to care for a Cadillac of any kind, and so my Barbies ended up with hideous double chins, a result of the frequent beheadings I would administer in order to marvel at the little round ball at the top of their neck. When I tried to put the head back on, it always got square and misshapen, leaving a perfect ten body with the head of Jabba the Hutt. I was basically a factory for Butterface Barbies in the mid- to late 1980s.

My friend Adri also had a lot of Barbies, and for some reason she always named her Barbie "Michael" when we made up stories. Michael and my Barbie had a relationship that consisted of fighting over Ken (or my Donnie Wahlberg concert series NKOTB doll) and changing outfits approximately every five seconds. I didn't have this cultural reference at the time, but our Barbies were essentially Carrie Bradshaw if she had been given an elephant's dose of methamphetamines and locked in her closet. They got dressed, admired each other, changed clothes, sat down, swapped shoes and put on hats, and then decided to go shopping, which of course necessitated a dressing room montage. One time we decided that Michael would travel to Hawaii, only to be kidnapped by natives, who plotted to burn her passport and birth certificate. Michael, naturally, changed clothes to attend the bonfire ceremony.

Top 10 Most Shocking Revelations From My Barbies' Tell-All Memoirs, Had They Been Able to Write

1. Made to wear ball gown stained with cat urine for days on end, with no black-tie event in sight!

2. Forced to engage in frottage with Ken . . . and sometimes even Skipper.

3. Head repeatedly removed from body and roughly replaced, resulting in a shortened neck and unsightly double chin.

4. Hamsters allowed to defecate in "Dream House."

5. Toes hacked off using childproof scissors: "I just wanted to die."

6. Crudely scalped with safety scissors; hair never grew back.

7. Once left naked and facedown in Barbie Puppy Water Park pool for over an hour during family barbecue.

8. Ken more interested in wardrobe changes than in sex.

9. Unable to walk in heels ever since both kneecaps were inverted.

10. Never *once* called by Christian name, Barbara.

My affections for Barbie waned when I brought home Jem. Jem, apart from being truly, truly, truly outrageous, was also larger in scale than Barbie, so much so that I could not play with the two of them at the same time, because Jem ended up looking like Yao Ming. Since I didn't have any of the Hologram or Misfit dolls I decided the only thing to do was to make Jem into an outcast. I gave her a crude buzz cut using dull scissors that nipped off bits of her scalp. I then wrote on her face with my purple gel pen, most notably a forehead tattoo that read, simply, FUCK. The Barbies retreated (possibly to Hawaii to reunite with Michael) and I soon tired of playing with a doll that resembled a cross between Sinead O'Connor and Charles Manson.

Part II, 1990s

An Embarrassment of Lists

My parents have saved every single thing I ever made for them—hand-drawn cards, pipe cleaner necklaces, pencil holders made from toilet paper rolls, unidentifiable ceramic orbs weighing approximately twelve pounds each (mug? paperweight? shot put?)—and so it makes sense that they have carefully cataloged and filed all my Christmas and birthday wish lists over the years. When viewed as a collection, they speak volumes.

The first artifact can be scientifically dated to within one year of 1990.

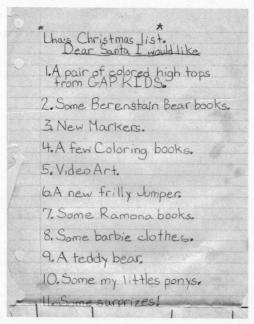

Lhas Christmas list.
Dear Santa I would like
1. A pair of colored high tops from GAP KIDS.
2. Some Berenstain Bear books.
3. New Markers.
4. A few Coloring books.
5. Video Art.
6. A new frilly Jumper.
7. Some Ramona books.
8. Some barbie clothes.
9. A teddy bear.
10. Some my littles ponys.
11. Some surprizes!

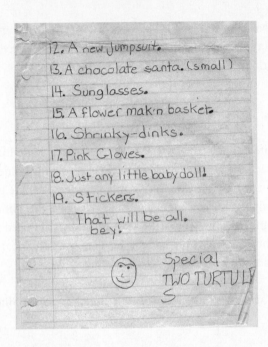

Note that there are *nineteen* separate items and then a dismissive "That will be all."

A year later, fewer items but more editorial notes.

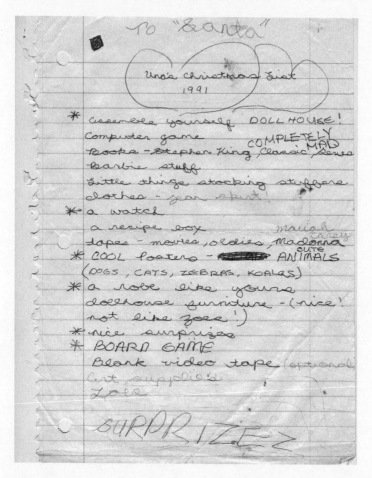

Dear "Santa," the jig is up! Knowing my parents would be doing the shopping, I took liberties with my editorial comments. "COOL Posters" are specified as "Dogs, Cats, Zebras, Koalas" and next to "dollhouse furniture" I demanded "nice!!! not like Zoe's!!!" (Incidentally, I would receive an Assemble-Your-Own Dollhouse and would abandon it half-finished, true to form.)

Not long after, I discovered troll dolls.

UNA'S BIRTHDAY LIST - 1992

(You do not have to get all things on this list. Things I especially want are marked with *.)

* 1. <u>Books</u> - Stephen King - THE SHINING, SKELETON CREW, FIRE STARTER, NEEDFUL THINGS, CUJO, ETC.

         Ann M. Martin - STACEY AND THE MYSTERY OF STONYBROOK, JESSI AND THE DANCE SCHOOL PHANTOM, DAWNS BIG SLEEPOVER, JESSIS WISH. ALSO MYSTERY #2,

3.

         Alfred Hitchcock, Twilight Zone type stories. SPELLBINDERS!!!!!!!
Sweet Valley Twins & High books

* 2. <u>Barbies</u> - Totally Hair Barbie

         Benetton Barbie

         Barbie acessories!!!

         Babysitter Club Doll

3. <u>Tapes</u> - Madonna, Mariah Carey, C&C Music Factory

* 4. <u>My Own Stationary</u> - Not my design. Professional like daddy's.

* 5. Crazy Earrings and Odds and Ends - Jewelry, Stickers, Paper Dolls, Pens & Pencils

* 6. SURPRISES!!!!!!!!!!!!

**** 7. TROLLS!!!!!! - Big trolls, little trolls, every kind of troll!!!!! I LOVE Trolls!!! I Want Lots!!!!

         Yours truly,

         Una C. Lamarche - K.I.D

In this list—my first using a computer—the Notorious K.I.D. helpfully informed her parents that they did not need to get everything she asked for and marked things she *really* needed with an asterisk. (Or, in the case of troll dolls, four asterisks and six exclamation points.)

As I entered adolescence, my lists reflected the sorts of poor choices brought on by hormone imbalances and exposure to sanctimonious teen soap operas.

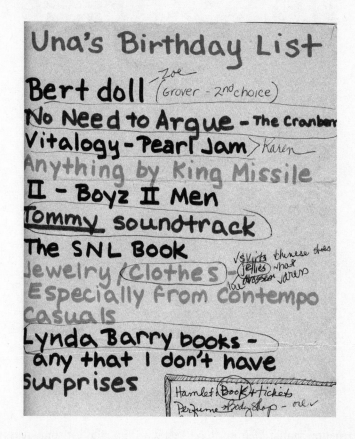

Una's Birthday List
Bert doll —Zoe (Grover - 2nd choice)
No Need to Argue - The Cranber
Vitalogy - Pearl Jam > Karen
Anything by King Missile
II - Boyz II Men
Tommy soundtrack
The SNL Book
Jewelry (Clothes) - chinese shoes / jellies / jeans
Especially from Contempo
Casuals
Lynda Barry books -
any that I don't have
Surprises
Hamlet Book & tickets
Perfume #Body Shop - one

No one but me knows that I asked for the Pearl Jam CD just so I could say I owned it. "Anything by King Missile," "Especially from Contempo Casuals" . . . I have no explanation for these sentences except for surging hormones. I don't remember why I wanted a Bert doll, but I'm guessing it was a stab at the first ironic recognition of my unibrow.

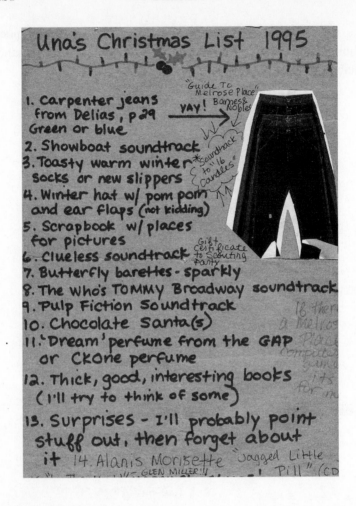

Una's Christmas List 1995

1. Carpenter jeans from Delias, p 29 Green or blue — yay! "Guide To Melrose Place" Barnes & Nobles
2. Showboat soundtrack — *soundtrack to "16 Candles"*
3. Toasty warm winter socks or new slippers
4. Winter hat w/ pom pom and ear flaps (not kidding)
5. Scrapbook w/ places for pictures
6. Clueless soundtrack — Gift Certificate to Scouting Party
7. Butterfly barettes - sparkly
8. The Who's TOMMY Broadway soundtrack
9. Pulp Fiction Soundtrack
10. Chocolate Santa(s)
11. "Dream" perfume from the GAP or CKone perfume
12. Thick, good, interesting books (I'll try to think of some)
13. Surprises - I'll probably point stuff out, then forget about it 14. Alanis Morisette "Jagged Little Pill" (CD

Carpenter jeans! *Melrose Place*! Yes, it's 1995, and for some reason I really want sparkly butterfly barrettes. Because they go so well with carpenter jeans and a hat with pom-poms and earflaps while jamming to the *Showboat* soundtrack. (Kidding this time! Kidding.) *N.B. Lists from 1996 to 1999 are nowhere to be found, which I can only assume means that they committed seppuku in order to protect what remains of my honor.*

~

Part III, 2000s

Decade of Buyer's Remorse

~

In 2002 I graduated from college, and in 2003 I got my first credit card, two events that ushered in an exciting new era in which I attempted to soothe my postcollege angst by purchasing everything and anything I could get my hands on. Giving a high credit limit to any twentysomething is a gamble, but giving one to a person who used to spend all her allowance money on as much candy as she could cram into her mouth on her five-minute walk home from school is called *enabling*. In fact, if I could change one thing about my life, I would not erase my unibrow or advise my thirteen-year-old self not to use scented hand cream as a tampon lubricant. No, I would go back and destroy my American Express card. Because I am still, to this day, paying off mistakes that include but are not limited to the following:

Label maker, November 2002. Oh, label maker. Throughout elementary school I coveted you. When I went to friends' houses and discovered they owned you, I would sneak quick trysts with you in the guest bathroom, printing out short labels like SOCKS and CANDY, for a planned organizational system I learned from the Berenstain Bear books that involved a lot of shoe boxes. But once I actually possessed you, I found I had a lot less to label than I thought I did. Mainly because I do not yet have Alzheimer's, and I already know where I keep my 2010 tax return, spare expired pregnancy tests, and family-size Twizzlers without having to be reminded.

Brazilian bikini wax, April 2003. I should have known it was a bad idea when the lady waxer looked horrified when I told her she was my first. "You never had regular bikini wax and you're getting Brazilian?" she asked incredulously. But I was adamant. It was a birthday present to myself, the kind you can only get with a straight face when you are twenty-three and single. It. Hurt. Also I started sleeping with my now-husband a few weeks afterward and he informed me that my nether region looked "like an exclamation point." (!)

Pants, 2003 to 2009 (online only). If you take one thing away from this book, I want it to be that you should never, under any circumstances, order pants online. *That is a fool's game.*

Adorable pilgrim shoes I couldn't afford from Anthropologie, March 2006. I know. I *know.* Pilgrim shoes? Gurrrl, *no.* But I promise they were really, really cute. They had low heels and a sassy front flap with a button and they made me feel like a sexy librarian from the 1960s (or, okay, maybe 1690s). They were also two hundred dollars, and they broke within two months.

Pottery Barn monogrammed whiskey decanter, December 2008. (See page 108.)

~

Part IV, 2010s

Drugstore Betrayal

~

Now that I'm in my thirties and have a child, most of my purchases are of a practical nature, even though as a kid I distinctly remember watching my parents ooh and aah over dish towels and historical novels they received as gifts and making a mental note:

Stay cool, self. Don't be that guy. Always *demand amazing toys and salacious Hollywood autobiographies!*

But age has a way of humbling you, and also I legitimately want socks for Christmas. I don't see why this is so hard for my inner child to accept.

Of course, there are times when I look down into my weeknight drugstore basket and see my merchandise the way a stranger might, nothing more than a depressing sum of its parts—like the time I stood in line behind a man in a West Texas Walmart as he bought a loaf of white bread and a box of bullets. I judged him then, but are a bottle of Drano and a discount double-feature DVD of Tom Hanks movies really any better?

Hey! these items say, *I enjoy bathing my seventeen cats while sobbing uncontrollably to '90s romantic comedies!*

Or: *Cutting locks of my own hair to send to Tom Hanks has really done a number on my drain!*

At least I wasn't also buying condoms. I know I should be cool about it by now, but no matter how old I get, buying condoms is *never* not embarrassing.

First you have to find the condom aisle, which is different in every drugstore (in the worst cases, they are stored right in front of the pharmacist, who stands there and watches as you silently weigh the pros and cons of ultrathin vs. ribbed). If there is some-

one already standing in the condom aisle but *not* buying condoms (say, a fresh-faced teenager perusing the feminine hygiene products or an elderly man looking for Gold Bond . . . *hypothetically*) you have to stand there pretending to look at something else and wait them out. By buying a box of condoms you are announcing to all strangers in view: *I am planning to have sex soon.* If you linger before choosing, you are announcing: *I am deciding what specific type of sex I am going to be having soon.*

Of course, worse than strangers not buying condoms are strangers who *are* buying condoms. Right next to you. Standing next to a stranger in front of the condoms is not only saying, *I am planning to have sex soon.* It is saying, *We are* both *planning to have sex soon.* And if one or both of you have penises, you have to send out extra brain-wave messages to any other strangers who might be watching: *This is not the person I will be having sex with soon. Why would we buy twenty-four condoms just for today? That is clearly too much. Even for a nymphomaniac. Which I am not. He might be, though. Who knows? Ha-ha-ha. Please kill me.*

Then, once you finally have your condoms and have fled the aisle, you must check out. You are forced to actually *hand* the condoms to the checkout person. *Here,* you are saying. *These are the condoms I have chosen with which to have sex soon. One of them will soon be in contact with my genitals. Please hold it for me while I look for my wallet.*

⁀

Condoms and Drano are actually among my more exciting purchases these days. The child who once demanded a make-your-own-dollhouse kit that she started and promptly put aside in order to tattoo her Barbies with obscenities must be weeping at the fact that I will gladly drop one hundred times her weekly allowance on an ergonomic desk chair, or that my Christmas lists now include acupuncture treatments, with as many exclamation points as I once reserved for troll dolls.

But I like to think I learned something over the intervening years—something that certainly does not require thousands of dollars of credit card debt or a closetful of ill-fitting pants to absorb. The things that make me truly happy can't be bought, at least not outside of an illegal black market or Harry Potter wizard store. My husband. My son. Thunderstorms. Shooting stars. Sleeping in. The ocean on a cloudy day. A flattering sailor suit for a woman.

Some things are just too beautiful to be owned.

The Unfairness of Life, Expressed by Venn Diagram

Hair looks decent

Face okay

Only clean clothes = harem pants, pocket square

No.

Picasso's "Seated Figure, Cystic Acne"

Follicular betrayal

Not wearing bathing suit bottoms as underpants

Designer Impostor

My husband, Jeff, and I share a pair of sweatpants. On me they are big and roomy; on him they are as tight as '70s gym clothes. For me they are sleeping sweatpants and eating sweatpants, and every fourth Monday or so they are my half-assed yoga-DVD-doing sweatpants. For Jeff they are his playing-my-nerdy-war-game-on-the-Internet sweatpants and also his I-don't-feel-like-putting-on-underwear sweatpants. Sometimes they are my I-don't-feel-like-putting-on-underwear sweatpants, too. We both go commando in these sweatpants, often without washing in between. And yes, since you ask, the magic *is* gone.

I don't think there is a more perfect item of clothing than sweatpants. They are stretchy and comfy and perfect for all occasions. Or at least, they will be

You can wipe those tears of jealousy away. I'll wait.

once the genius who popularized formal shorts finds a way to market formal sweats (come on, asshole, *you owe us*).

My very first pair of sweatpants made me so happy that I wore them for first-grade picture day.

My next pair of sweatpants was my so-called "warm-up" sweats for high school track. Underneath them I wore tiny shorts made of factory-rejected Glad Cling Wrap, which was an added incentive not to ever take them off. Long after I quit track I kept my sweatpants. They came with me to college. They absorbed the smoke from my first joint and did not judge me when I gained ten pounds in my first semester (probably a direct result of the entire blocks of cheddar cheese I would consume while stoned). They became my study sweatpants and then, senior year, my mourning sweatpants when I first got my heart broken for real. The summer after college I cropped them, because nothing is sexier than cropped, saggy sweatpants. I took to wearing them to the corner bodega with tank tops and those flimsy Chinese slippers, and as I stood at the register clutching my toilet paper and Cheez Doodles, I noticed that not even the old men sitting outside on milk crates with their ten a.m. beers were looking at me. They became my invisibility sweatpants. My freedom sweatpants, if you will. One day, under circumstances that I have since forgotten or blocked out, I discovered that I could pull the elastic waist up over my boobs and create a strapless, cropped-sweat unitard. I wore it on my first date with Jeff.

Kidding. He *wishes*.

I don't have any photos of these magical sweatpants, because they were too awesome. Their beauty could not be captured on film. When a hole began to form in the crotch circa 2007 I thought, *Yesssss, now I don't even have to take them off to pee!* What I didn't realize is that it also meant I couldn't wear them to greet the Thai deliveryman anymore. Eventually, and with great sadness, I got rid of them. Which brings me to my marital sweatpants.

Jeff bought them a few years ago, for himself, foolishly think-ing that I would not fall in love with them. They're not much to look at—gray, bulky, nondescript but for an Old Navy logo on the left hip—but they are lined with cozy, fleecelike cotton and when I put them on they sink down to the floor, pooling around my feet so that it looks like I'm melting. The baggy hips conceal even the most egregious PMS bloat, and I could probably walk out of a grocery store with five pounds of potatoes hidden in the soft, elephant-like folds of the ass. They are my clothing nirvana.

$\frown$

I'm telling you this not for the evocative mental images, but rather to underscore the point that I don't belong anywhere near high fashion. It isn't that I have *no* style—I had a rocky adolescence, sure, but Jeff recently described my look as "the neurotic best friend character in a mid-'90s rom-com," the highest compliment I have been given to date. It's more that, while I covet clothing, I can't shake my deep belief that the fashion industry is, for lack of a better word, dumb. I know: there goes my *Vogue* profile. But it's probably for the best, as my sole pair of designer shoes was stained a fetching shade of brown after I donned them to stomp through mud at a friend's rustic wedding, and now they look as if I wore them for an *America's Next Top Model* challenge that required me to climb—fiercely!—out of a porta-potty. Also, I can't pronounce a lot of the high-end brand names. When I try to say Proenza Schouler, it sounds like I'm having a stroke. And, hey, Monique Lhuillier: is it *Lull-ee-yay*? *Loo-lee-yer*? *Lwee-lee-air*? I guess you can't just go by Monique because of Mo'Nique, huh?

But I digress. The sad truth is that although my fashion history includes a silk tapestry-print vest worn backward in honor of Kris Kross, I love clothes. I *loooooove* them. Not just the ones made out of performance fleece, either; someday, I aspire to own things that I call "pieces" because they are classic and tailored, not because they're secretly held together with staples. And, like any normal woman who has been conditioned by the media to hate herself deeply and who turns to retail therapy in the hopes of finding that one elusive purchase that will heal her pain forever (and also maybe make people mistake her for a taller Natalie Portman), I spend a truly astounding amount of time fantasizing about the wardrobe I would have if I (a) had the money and (b) had the kind of grace that would ensure that none of my pants could ever be described using phrases like "oatmeal encrusted" or "wet around the crotch area for unknown reasons."

Pie Chart of My Shirt Drawer at 33 Years Old

- Shirts purchased from Etsy, bearing likeness of Shannen Doherty or a member of NKOTB
- "Sleep shirts," a.k.a. shirts not to be worn outside of home* due to state of disrepair/ unfortunate slogan
- (*regularly worn outside of home)
- Stained maternity tops—still in heavy rotation!
- Pants
- Passable top-half clothing for an adult

I fully identify with fashion's allure, and I appreciate its ability to transform; without fashion, after all, there would be no makeover shows, which would be a travesty, because I get a nice dopamine buzz whenever someone walks out from behind a curtain in a tasteful pencil skirt and her family gasps and cries. Also, no one would ever use the word "reveal" as a noun. I don't have a problem with people wanting to look better and feel good about themselves. I do, however, have a problem with people (specifically women) feeling pressure to look like sixteen-year-old Ukrainian models.

And this is where my problem with the fashion industry really comes into play. Because the way it's set up now, a small group of the extremely wealthy creates inordinately expensive clothes that are overwhelmingly made to flatter clothes hangers. That's not a slur I made up for models, by the way; I'm being literal. I once read a piece in a fashion magazine in which a designer was actually *quoted* as saying that the average body distorted the shape of clothes, and that they were designed to hang beautifully, not cling stubbornly to, you know, actual human flesh. Imagine if someone said that about a car: "Sorry, a 'real' body kind of interrupts the flow of the dashboard, ma'am. Is there maybe an underfed child who could drive this instead of you?"

Then there's the fallacy that fashion lets you express your true self. I mean, sure it does, if you accept the fact that someone else is deciding for you who you should want to be. Every season, there are trends that trickle down the totem pole, from Prada to J.Crew to Lane Bryant to Walmart. (I like to think it's the fashion equivalent of a papal conclave, involving Anna Wintour and the Olsen twins, and that everyone wears *Star Trek* glasses and plays air guitar like those futuristic elders in *Bill and Ted's Excellent Adventure*.) All of a sudden, everyone is inexplicably dying for tartan jeggings or neon midirompers or the sturdy orthopedic sandals my mom's elderly Polish cleaning lady wears. (That last example actually happened for the entire summer of 2011, and I saw them recently on Dakota Fanning. *Dakota Fanning!*) So consumers, regardless of their finances, end up looking more or less alike, and yet supposedly everyone is simultaneously expressing their unique and innermost soul sparkles. *This is what* The Matrix *was about, people.*

After reading the previous paragraphs, you might be thinking, *Hey, you seem pretty biased, lady. You habitually wear sweatpants out of doors. I don't think you should write about fashion, and also, I don't think you watched* The Matrix *very closely.* And you would be right.

But that didn't stop me from going to New York Fashion Week and getting doused in glitter confetti while close enough to high-five Joan Collins. Because through a series of errors in judgment (mostly mine but also Arianna Huffington's) I was, for a brief period circa 2010, considered a—wait for it—*fashion critic*. I didn't think I was even eligible for the title, seeing as I once owned and frequently wore a pair of salmon-colored shortalls, but thanks to a stint recapping *Project Runway* for the *Huffington Post*, I currently have literally tens of people who care what I think about *style* (that's French for "style"). This makes me both a hypocrite and a terrible role model. But it is a fact that Tim Gunn once complimented my sandals, so here are some professional fashion tips, from me to you. . . .

How to Look Like a Semipresentable Adult at Least Most of the Time, by Noted Fashion Critic / Human Clothes Hanger Una LaMarche

Don't Try to Look Like a Sailor

First of all, I don't know who decided that wearing white pants was a thing. Unless you live inside a Ralph Lauren ad among nothing but sun-bleached rocks and immaculately scrubbed yacht decks, in a land where everyone is freshly waxed and possessed of a bounty of flan-colored thongs, white pants are not your friend. Secondly, anchors add about eighteen pounds, depending on the size of your boat (not a euphemism). Finally and most importantly, not even sailors look that good dressed as sailors. You* credit *On the Town* for your sexual awakening without realizing that Frank Sinatra and Gene Kelly are sexy because *they're Frank Sinatra and Gene Kelly*, not because of their dress whites. Remember that third guy? The much-less-attractive one? How did that little diaphragm hat look on him? The prosecution rests.

Tell "Dry-Clean Only" It Can Go Dry-Fuck Itself

Fact: no one actually understands the process of dry cleaning. The cool hanger carousel totally sells it, and we fork over twelve dollars to clean a forty-dollar sweater, because the all-caps label ordered us to.

I like to picture dry cleaning as some combination of *Breaking Bad*'s meth lab and an antigravity chamber, in which clothes spin suspended in midair as the stains lift off like flights of doves made from a sludge of red wine and cake frosting. But no. A quick Google search reveals that dry cleaning happens inside a

*I.

machine that looks suspiciously *exactly like a washing machine*, filled with chemicals that are decidedly *wet*. Hmm-mm. Simple coincidence, or massive con job? Before you decide, I'll leave you with this nugget of dry-cleaning history from Wikipedia (emphasis mine):

> The ancient Romans used ammonia (derived from urine) . . . to launder their woolen togas. . . . These laundries obtained urine from farm animals, or from special pots situated at public latrines.

Listen, designers, if I could clean my formalwear with pee, I'd do my own laundry at home while taking a shower. Put *that* on your label and dry it.

Rethink the Basics

While trends come and go, the general fashion consensus seems to be that every stylish woman needs a small selection of well-tailored, neutral, presumably "dry-clean only" staples. Surely you've read a fashion magazine article or two hundred describing in evangelical rapture the virtues of things like a sexy yet conservative black sheath dress, the "perfect" white button-down blouse, a pencil skirt tight enough to double as a gastric band, or a classic wool peacoat.

I own none of these things. Instead, my closet is a Muppet-colored rainbow of impulse purchases that never paid off: the hot pink Betsey Johnson miniskirt so short it barely clears my labia, found on fire sale for twelve dollars; the purple harem pants that look like something Grimace would wear to a Turkish bathhouse; the glittery bolero that makes me look less like a flamenco dancer and more like a flamboyant Amtrak conductor. When I need to dress for something that requires an air of gravitas—say, a work meeting or a funeral—I

have to go shopping, and inevitably, while searching for an appropri-
ately grown-up item, my eyes fall upon a festive poncho or a pair of
bright yellow track pants, and the cycle starts anew.

I have accepted that I will never be the type of lady who owns
something presentable in the color beige or who can walk more
than a few steps in a pair of four-inch heels or who matches her
bra with her underwear more than five percent of the entire calendar year (and only then by accident). But I have come up with
a revised list of basic purchases that can prevent people like me
from experiencing frequent sartorial shame in the face of non-
Halloween events:

Women:

- 1 pair fitted jeans, low-rise enough so that you can eat
  a whole pizza and still feel good about your legs
- 10 of the most flattering cheap T-shirts you can find,
  in colors that run the gamut from "papal audience" to
  "Pride Week"
- 1 knee-length shirtdress that makes you feel like an
  impossibly fetching librarian
- 1 nice dress that does not require constant boob shift-
  ing or more than one pair of Spanx, and also does not
  incorporate any of the following into its design: giant
  chest rosette; feathers; sparkle belt; ombré; chain print
- 1 pair cute flats you can walk twenty miles in
- 1 pair boots you can wear with both dresses and jeans
- 1 pair dressy heels that don't give you bunions, flesh
  wounds, or scoliosis
- 1 purse that can hold both a book and a sandwich

Men:

- 1 pair dark jeans *not* large enough to conceal a canned
  ham (not a euphemism) in any area

- 1 suit that makes you do a sexy James Bond pose
  when you look in the mirror
- At least 3 T-shirts with no writing, artwork (this category *includes tie-dye*), team or brand name of any
  kind, anywhere
- 1 button-down shirt with no visible stains
- 1 classy V-neck sweater (trust me)
- 1 pair sneakers
- 1 pair dress shoes
- 0 pairs Adidas slip-on shower sandals

Everything else is just gravy.

Embrace the Granny Panty

I harbor the delusion that I might, at any time, in any place, be required to strip down to my underwear. This belief is the driving
force behind my daily selection of lingerie. *Better not wear the
threadbare Hanes with all the crotch holes,* I think, furrowing my
brow. *Just on the off chance that the FBI raids Ye Olde Bagel Shoppe
while I'm waiting for a cronut and needs to check if I'm wearing a wire.*

In my defense, this has actually happened once. Not the FBI
cronut part, but having to strip down to my skivvies without prior
notice. It was a night of after-work drinking that took an especially drunken turn and ended up at an indoor pool in the lobby
of a Times Square hotel. It was not one of the eighteen days a year
that I managed to coordinate underwear patterns, so I was rocking
a black bra and a red bathing suit bottom, a choice that under
other circumstances (FBI, cronut) might have been embarrassing
but which actually proved useful in this instance since I was, in
fact, swimming (or, at least, sitting in water, drinking Jameson).
Also, it turned out to be Gay Night at the swim-up bar, so no one
even glanced in my direction. All in all, it was a triumph, assum-

ing you don't count the fact that I threw up in my purse on the subway ride home.

This obsession with being intimately prepared should a sexy EMT have to cut me out of my clothes to administer a defibrillator led me to shun comfort briefs—i.e., the "granny panty"—until very recently. Maybe it's that I had a baby; once you have three or more people staring directly into your taint as a human head fights its way out of the birth canal, I guess being seen in *any* underwear looks pretty good by comparison. Or maybe it's just that they're like genital sweatpants: comfy, dependable, and devoid of any artifice or pretense. Whatever it is, I love them. And I'm not afraid to say it.

There is no other piece of clothing that gets as little respect as the GP, but grannies have a lot to teach us. They still practice proper penmanship and send handwritten thank-you notes. They can make everything from chocolate chip cookies to roast beef without consulting a cookbook, let alone the Internet. They don't recognize "the Situation" as a person and wisely stay away from jeggings. So why not follow their lead when it comes to undergarment selection?

I already know what you're going to say. The granny panty is notorious for being a sexual deal-breaker. Legend has it that if a paramour rips your dress off to reveal a pair of waist-high, Band-Aid-colored briefs, he or she will recoil in disgust and leave you to weep into your Häagen-Dazs along with your seventeen cats. But, ladies, show me someone who gets as far as your panties and then decides to call it a night, and I will show you someone who is either unconscious or not attracted to people of your gender.

I fell in love with the GP while pregnant, for its full and forgiving coverage of my expanding assets (something no one tells you: when you're pregnant your growing belly pulls your pubic hairline up a good two inches). But I love them even when I'm not carrying an extra forty pounds, and here's why:

1. They're roomy. Like drop-crotch pants, I imagine, but less embarrassing to wear in public.
2. They're comforting. The granny panty is to the vagina what sweatpants are to the legs, or mac and cheese is to the stomach, assuming you're not lactose intolerant.
3. They're trendy. Yes, I said trendy. What are Spanx if not unnaturally tight granny panties? Think about it.

Sure, Sisqo never wrote a song about them, but is that really a bad thing? Embrace the space. Respect the stretch. Lose the scanty panty. Grandma knows best.

Read Fashion Magazines with a Sense of Humor

I have a love/hate relationship with women's magazines. I love how thick and glossy they are, filling my mailbox with the intoxicating scent of perfume and the promise of a lazy afternoon spent looking at candy-colored baubles and the freakishly static planes of Nicole Kidman's face. But I hate how vapid they can be, assuming that women don't appreciate wit or sarcasm, pretending that we don't notice that they just publish the same fucking "Easy Summer Beauty" or "No-Diet Diet" articles every single issue with different pictures, and assuming that if they were to run a single photo of a real woman or plus-size model it would undo all the subtle hate-your-body messages they've been sending for decades.

Sometimes, though, if you look for it, they are hilarious. I have taken the liberty of penning a literal explanation of one particularly choice headline:

How to Wear a White Shirt (June 2010 *Allure*)

1. Go to closet; open it.
2. Pick out a shirt (the item of clothing with no legs that isn't

long enough to cover your ass) that is not red, orange, yellow, green, blue, indigo, violet, black, brown, pink, or any of the aforementioned colors in pastel. Also avoid prints. Pick something the color of clouds, only not rain clouds . . . or sunset-reflecting clouds. Hmm, that could get confusing. Okay, pick something the color of fresh fallen snow that has not been peed on.

3. Does the shirt button up the front? In that case put your arms in the holes and then fasten all the buttons. If there are no buttons, stick your head in the top hole and your arms in the side holes and pull the front down over your chest and stomach.

4. Oh, wait, do you have breasts? If so, reverse step 3 and put on a bra first. Since your shirt is white, your bra must be that fetching shade of beige that recalls leftover flan, in order not to show through.

5. Ta-da! You're done. Except for pants, which will be discussed in next month's issue.

Stop Before You Drop or Crop

You may remember near the beginning of this story that I mentioned having once cropped my high school track sweats, thus turning something with a natural drop-crotch into a crop-drop-crotch pant. And it's frankly amazing I'm even alive to type this, since it's the fashion equivalent of staring into a dark bathroom mirror and shouting "Bloody Mary" thirteen times.

Let's start with crop tops. People who wear them are shameless braggarts. First of all, they're mocking those of us with a strong nostalgic affection for the fashion of the early 1990s, but more important, they are choosing to highlight—out of all possible exposed flesh on the human body—the abdominals, which is probably collectively our worst feature. Historically, the abdomen helps us breathe, stand up reasonably straight, cough, poop, and sing. It does not need to win any beauty contests, and it definitely does not need to look like a relief map of the Rocky Mountains. If you want to show off your abs, go to the beach.

Next: cropped pants. These are less offensive, but have you really ever met anyone over age eleven whose legs look great cut off midcalf? Here's a test: Google "Angelina Jolie capri pants" and you will not find a single image.

On to drop-crotch pants: Justin Bieber apparently suffers from elephantiasis of the testes, or else he requires a colostomy bag, I don't know. Seriously, drop-crotch pants, what is your game? What are you hiding in there? Adult diapers? Vestigial tails? Crowning babies? Look, I get it; my mom always told me my vagina needed to breathe (which was really confusing before I realized she was being figurative), but I didn't know I needed to stow an iron lung down there.

In fact, might I suggest—if you're in the market for extra crotch room *and* require the ability to move both legs at once—a pair of fleece-lined, extra-large Old Navy brand sweatpants? They can be had for a pittance, yet savored for a lifetime.

JEAN SHORTS: A ~~USER'S~~ LOSER'S GUIDE

The only hard-and-fast rule I know about summer clothing is that it's okay to wear white shoes only between Memorial Day and Labor Day.

I don't know who decided this—probably the same old rich dudes who find it acceptable to attend yacht parties wearing pastel-colored khakis embossed with tiny lobsters and schooners.

Anyway, the white-shoe thing isn't even a problem for me, because wearing white shoes in New York City is a dangerous game. After a week, your virginal footwear will take on the fetching, mottled gray hue of diseased pigeon (incidentally one of New York's most prized indigenous species).

My summer style conundrum can be summed up in two words: jean shorts. I love jean shorts . . . in theory. In *theory*, as soon as I put them on I look like Gisele Bündchen from the waist down. In *theory*, my skin turns from the color of tracing paper to the color of fine scotch, and my legs grow two feet, like Inspector Gadget's do when he needs to climb over tall things. But this is all in *theory*. In reality, even doing my modeliest pose I resemble an albino Munchkin when compared to Her Leggyness. And in those photos I'm wearing *store-bought* jean shorts. So you can imagine how dire the situation is when I wear cutoffs I made myself. Wait, you know what? Why bother imagining? Let me show you.

Seriously, this is what a combined photo of the two of us would look like, to scale.

OH NO, SHE *DIY*-DN'T!
(JEAN SHORTS MISTAKES TO AVOID)

Please note: lest you think I've succumbed to TTDT (Thighs That Don't Touch) disease, know that I'm purposefully standing with my legs apart in these photos, for vanity purposes.

Chastity Shorts

Paranoid about accidentally cutting too short (see the Truck Stop Jailbait on page 148), you may end up with unflattering—albeit Vatican-appropriate—jean-Jams.

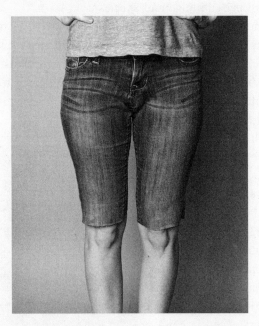

This is a hell-to-the-no style for all but the most coltish among us. Try again.

The Fraternal Twins

If you're anything like me, you don't use measuring tape or even a ruler; you just eyeball the length and hack away. This can result in an Arnold Schwarzenegger–Danny DeVito situation.

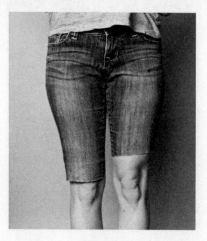

It can also result in . . .

The Mullet

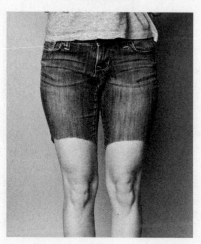

"Oh, hey!" you may be saying to yourself. "These look okay." But that is just your eyes deceiving you. Seen from a side angle, unscientific cutting has led to an uneven, Richard Dean Anderson effect.

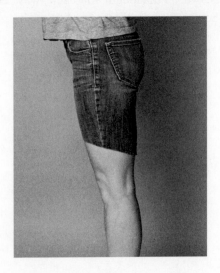

The Truck Stop Jailbait

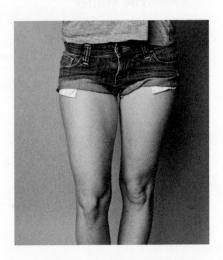

The only thing worse than leaving shorts too long is making the question "Who wears short shorts?" rhetorical.

(Fun story: I went to the NYC gay pride parade with my uncles in the mid-nineties, and a gentleman was wearing shorts so short his balls were hanging out of one side. Innocence lost!)

An Open Letter to Rompers

Hello, Rompers,

I saw you on the street today. A woman was wearing you. You were orange and strapless, with a not-insignificant boob ruffle. I glared at you as you passed, but you didn't notice. Then again, how could you? You were too busy multitasking. I'm sure that manifesting as a tube top *and* Daisy Dukes simultaneously takes its toll.

I shouldn't have been surprised to see you, but I wasn't prepared. When I first heard about you back in 2009, I thought, *Ha-ha-ha-ha, no way is that a thing. Someone at* Marie Claire *has been hitting the oxygen facials a little too hard. Surely no grown woman would willingly wear a garment defined as "a loosely fitted one-piece having short bloomers that is worn especially by small children for play."* But then Blake Lively showed up in you at a formal event and I knew it was over.

Last summer, I thought maybe you'd relent. I hoped against hope that some other trend would replace you—perhaps Anthropologie color-blocked lederhosen, old-timey unitard bathing suits, or full-body vajazzling accessorized with those shoes Lady Gaga favors that have no heel and appear to be crafted from vinyl-covered ox hooves. But no. You came back stronger than ever.

I'd find myself fondling what I thought was a dress in Forever 21 only to recoil in horror as my fingers stumbled upon a crotch seam. I confessed my despair to my husband, who seemed supportive until we happened across a frilly lavender version of you while on vacation. You were on sale. "We're buying this," my husband declared gleefully. He made me wear you defiantly as he snapped photos. I left you at the beach rental "by accident."

So forgive me, but when I saw you today I was taken aback. When are you planning on leaving, exactly? It's been six years now. Will you not rest until every American woman has to get fully naked in order to use the bathroom? Until babyGap is forced to expand its "onesies" section to include plus sizes? Until Blake Lively wets herself at the Teen Choice Awards? O Rompers, Rompers. *Wherefore art thou, Rompers?* Deny thy unitard and refuse thy belts.

You've overstayed your welcome. It's time for you to take your spaghetti straps and your fluttery leg holes and go back to toddlers where you belong.

Love,
Una

Free to Be Poo and Pee

A Guide to Public Restroom Usage for Classy Ladies

I pride myself on doing things "better" than everyone else, and this extends to peeing in public bathrooms. Like any normal person, I take my time when in the comfort of a private space, but when there's a line (or even when there *might* be another person waiting when I get out, as in a restaurant), I perform the equivalent of urinary wind sprints. After waiting ten minutes for the lady in front of me to create a batch of carefully brewed artisanal pee, I enter the stall like a contestant on *Supermarket Sweep*, in and out in sixty seconds. It's time, as mature women of the world, that we all got potty trained.

Before you get defensive, I'm not suggesting that everyone should race through the motions. You could sprain your groin or—worse!—get pee on the seat. But a little self-awareness never hurt anyone. So I'm going to share with you my three tenets for efficient and respectful ladies' room usage:

1. Speed
2. Cleanliness
3. Common Fucking Sense

Speed

Like I just said, there is no need to aim for my unique and freakish devotion to bathroom time trials. However, a public restroom—*especially* one that accommodates only one person at a time—is not the place to sit and contemplate your thoughts or show off your penis-etching skills. We all know that women only poop in public bathrooms under duress (more on this in a minute), so I'm going to assume that this is a "number one" situation. Go ahead and enjoy the release. Let it out. But as soon as it's over, *get up* and *get moving*. Wash your hands, dry them, and *go*. This is not the time for reapplying foundation or texting your sister. A quick mirror check for visible stains or missing teeth, a swipe of lip balm, and a blot with a paper towel and you should be out the door.

Cleanliness

Women come in many shapes, sizes, and colors, but they come in only two kinds when they step into a public restroom: those who sit and those who hover.

I myself am a sitter, and I don't use those disposable toilet seat covers, either. My rationale is that if you just sit down, no bodily fluids will get on the seat, hence you will be much less likely to get herpes, or someone else's pee on your butt. *However*, I realize that people are very passionate about this issue, and I acknowledge that some women would sooner give Gary Busey a full-body massage than let their flesh touch a toilet seat used by strangers. Fine. Go to town. Layer six of those suckers on the seat. Hover 'til your thighs turn to jelly. But afterward, I want you to do me a favor: look at the toilet. Have the seat covers been flushed away, or are they still sitting there like a damp sofa cushion made of tissue? Are there droplets of pee on the seat? If this *was* a dreaded "number two" scenario, could the bowl be fairly classified as a brunette?

Did you just change a tampon, and, if so, would that be immediately apparent to anyone else?

If you answer yes to any of these questions, you are not done yet. Clean it up.

Common Fucking Sense

- Those toilet seat covers have a middle part. It should be torn away before use, unless your goal is to collect your golden bounty and share it with others via festive streams down the bowl and onto the floor.
- Locks. Use them, love them. I no more want to walk in on you than I want you to spend thirty seconds jiggling the door handle while I am trying to coax the last few droplets out so that they don't decide to make their appearance during a business meeting while I'm wearing a thong. Which brings me to . . .
- Locks. Know how they work. If the door will not open, it is locked. This means *ocupado*. Stand and wait your turn.

As for the dreaded deuce, from nine to five we act like we're born without colons, just like we try to convince our paramours that we were born without leg hair. But this doesn't save us from the psychological torture of navigating the ladies' room.

I'm speaking, of course, of the Poop Stall. Hear me out.

Let's say a public ladies' room has three stalls—pretty standard.

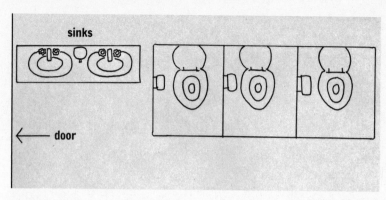

If a woman—let's call her Lady A—goes into an empty bathroom with three stalls she will always take the stall closest to the door. That way she can get out quickly if there is a freak toilet fire or a pack of assassins or—God forbid—Harry Connick Jr., waiting to strangle her with chicken wire (thanks a lot, *Copycat*, for giving us extra bathroom anxiety). The stall closest to the door also conveniently provides a buffer stall in the event that someone else comes in.

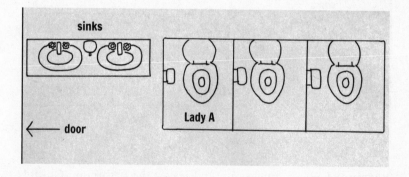

If Lady A is *pooping*, however, she will take the stall farthest from the door. It is just one of those inexplicable laws of nature, like gravity or neon frogs that kill you if you lick them.

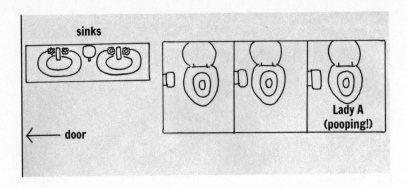

Let's assume, however, for the sake of argument, that Lady A is *not* pooping in this particular scenario. So she takes the first stall. Then, in comes Lady B. Lady B must take the Poop Stall, even though she is not pooping. The presence of another person already occupying the first stall temporarily lifts the stigma of the Poop Stall and it simply becomes the Stall That Is a Nonthreatening Distance from the Other Person in the Bathroom.

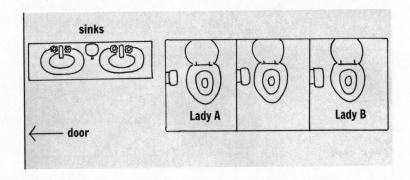

But wait! Lady A finishes up and leaves the bathroom. Oh no! Now Lady B is in the Poop Stall with no mitigating factor!

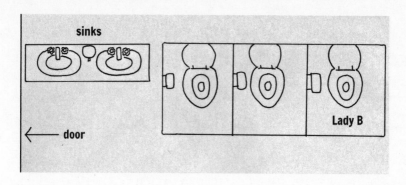

Then Lady C comes in. She sees Lady B in the Poop Stall and comes to the only rational conclusion, which is that Lady B is pooping. Lady B, at this point, is beside herself. This anxiety shuts off her urethra and prevents her from being able to audibly pee, which is even more damning.

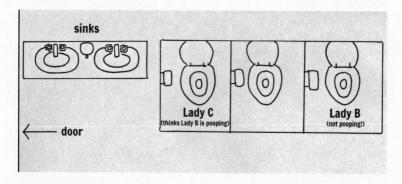

The only thing that can save Lady B now is a surprise appearance by Lady D, who takes the middle stall, thus restoring balance to the ladies' room ecosystem and neutralizing the tension between Ladies C and B (even though C still thinks B is pooping).

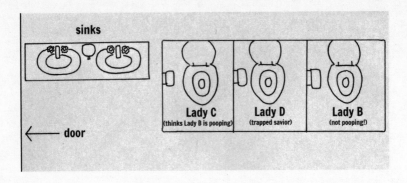

It's all very emotionally taxing. And that's not even taking into account four-stall models—which require a game plan worthy of a Division A college football team—or those vast airport bathrooms with literally endless rows of stalls that give them the feel of an M. C. Escher lithograph, albeit one that reeks of ammonia and urine.

Betty Friedan totally should have devoted a chapter in *The Feminine Mystique* to this.

Gullible's Travels

I like the idea of travel, but actually moving from one place to another has never been my favorite thing. As a child, I devoted a lot of time to designing an alternative mode of transportation I called "zapping."* Zapping would literally zap you into tiny invisible particles that would move you from wherever you happened to be to wherever you wanted to go with no physical effort on your part; the only rules were that you couldn't suddenly manifest in someone else's private space, and that there needed to be some physical indicator that a zapped person was about to appear so that people could move out of the way accordingly and not get into accidents. I decided that zapping time would depend somewhat on the distance traveled—zapping down to the kitchen would take a second, but zapping to Hong Kong from New York might last five minutes, and so for longer trips I designed a small vessel that resembled a private train car stocked with up-to-date magazines and candy. This was the beginning of the end. My overthinking spiraled out of control: hurtling through space at the speed of sound

---

*Science fiction aficionados might refer to this as "teleportation," but since I spent my leisure time listening to Garrison Keillor tapes instead of watching *Star Trek*, I believed I had come up with the concept.

would probably take a toll on the body, so a special suit might be necessary. And how many zaps at the same time could the universe accommodate without imploding? There would have to be a zap limit, or perhaps a zap tax. Zap insurance, for my own legal protection. Finally, I decided to just get off the couch and climb the twelve steps to the bathroom using my legs.

Unsurprisingly, given all this, I'm not the greatest companion for long-distance journeys. I get stressed out—possibly because no one has asked me to sing show tunes—and make bad decisions, like picking a fight with my husband in a fancy foreign restaurant, accidentally setting fire to curtains by placing them on a halogen lamp, trying to flush a poop-covered onesie down an airplane toilet, or using weird hotel soap on my vagina, which subsequently swells to four times its normal size.

But in the late spring of 2000, before I had a husband to fight with or a child whose bowels could explode at thirty-five thousand feet, I flew across the Atlantic to visit my friend Charlie in Regensburg, Germany, where he was taking a semester abroad. I emerged from that experience with a patch of electric orange hair and some valuable travel tips, such as the following.

Do Not Design an Entire Vacation Around the Ridiculous Hope That Your Gay Best Friend Will Make a Pass at You

This might seem obvious, but I suffer from a little-known condition called "reverse gaydar," in which I am powerfully attracted to men who prefer genitalia I do not possess. Also, this trip took place post–fake virginity loss but pre–*actual* virginity loss, so I was starting to feel desperate.

Study the Metric System in Advance

Two liters of anything is a lot to drink in one day, but if the thing you are drinking is beer, and the only things you are using to soak up the beer are half of a soft pretzel and forty light cigarettes, you will fall down. And if you are one of the only women in a gay dance club, and you are short and it is dark, no one will notice.

Don't Buy Hair Dye Abroad If the Instructions Are Not in Your Native Language; Also, Don't Bleach Hair While Intoxicated

Again, seems obvious until you have consumed two liters of beer and listened to a lot of Euro-trance sung by people who look like that little claymation elf Hermey from *Rudolph the Red-Nosed Reindeer*.

Don't Assume Your Whimsical Zest for Life Will Find You a Hotel Room

Charlie and I decided it would be fun to travel seven hours to Amsterdam by train in order to get really high. Our plan was to arrive in the afternoon, party through the night, and return the next day, sleeping only on the train. We thought this was an incredibly crafty way to save money on a hotel room, so we could use that money to buy more drugs.

Our first and perhaps most fatal mistake was forgetting that the drug we were planning on using was marijuana, more famous for inducing lethargy and increasing Pringles consumption than for its use as an energy booster. After the first "coffee shop" we stopped in, where we smoked two joints, we started to yawn. It was, after all, four p.m.

Next, we had neglected to consider the fact that even Amsterdam's bars had a last call. This fell at three a.m. I was already curled up on a banquette at the time, drifting in and out of consciousness, fantasizing about crawling into a bed, any bed, even one made of hay bales or previously slept on by Bret Michaels. Finally, Charlie stumbled over and dragged me upright.

"I'm *tiiiiiiiiiiiired*," I moaned.

"You're a little cupcake with feet," he said brightly. (Charlie was on magic mushrooms.)

"Can we find a hotel, please?"

"I saw one right outside!" He led me onto the dark cobblestone street and proudly gestured to a wooden bench littered with cigarette butts.

"That's not—" I started to say, but Charlie was already asleep.

We stayed there for about an hour, until the police came and yelled at us in Dutch.

Don't Try to Use European Bathroom Fixtures for Purposes They Were Not Designed For

By six thirty a.m., when we finally found a diner that was opening, I was exhausted and reeked of pot, well liquor, and sweat. So while Charlie ordered pancakes, I alighted to the bathroom to change clothes and try to take what is commonly called a "whore's bath," but which my mom always referred to as a "P.T.A.," which stands for "tits," "ass," and a word I would prefer not to hear my mother utter ever again. I added my hair to the menu of things to be washed, since it smelled like a night I never wanted to relive. So, half-naked, I bent my head into the tiny sink and drenched my scalp in freezing water. When I stood up to get some hand soap, I hit my head so hard on the underside of the faucet that I got vertigo and fell backward into the bidet.

Don't Smuggle Illegal Drugs Between Countries

As we were finishing our breakfast, Charlie suddenly remembered that he had promised to buy a brick of hash for his friend Ben, back in Germany. Now, I am someone who is made uncomfortable by taking empty seats with a better view at a baseball game, so the idea that I would be trafficking drugs across an international border sent me into paroxysms of anxiety. But I was too defeated to fight, and besides, Charlie suggested that since we'd be going to a "coffee shop" anyway, we might as well smoke some for the road. We were just full of great decisions.

Don't Let a High Person Hide the Drugs

Charlie had heard that stuffing marijuana into a jar of Nutella was a good tactic to avoid detection, since the thick, chocolate-hazelnut paste camouflaged any scent that might be picked up by a drug-sniffing dog. We purchased our Nutella, followed by the hash, followed by a few joints, and Charlie went into the men's room to do the deed. Twenty minutes later, he emerged looking like an outhouse had exploded on him.

"What *happened*?" I asked, blotting the remainder of the blood from my damp, stringy hair.

Charlie just shrugged and grinned. "I'm being pulled back by the universe," he said. (He had taken more mushrooms.)

We departed for the train, the very picture of stealth.

Amazingly, we made it back to Regensburg without killing each other or getting arrested, although Charlie reported that a German family had watched me sleeping with my mouth open and speculated that I might be mentally retarded.

Still, the unconsciousness made that the uncontested highlight of the trip.

Drinks on Me—No, Literally, *on* Me

Potential Pitfalls in the World of Potables

I have vomited into two purses, which, in the grand scheme of things, doesn't seem like that many.

After all, I've owned probably thirty purses since the brown LeSportsac bag I bought in tenth grade, which means that I've only vomited into one-fifteenth of my purses. This strikes me as respectable, probably somewhere in between Queen Elizabeth and Courtney Love.

I'd like to state for the record that both times I sacrificed handbags to the contents of my stomach I was in fact making clumsy attempts at politeness. The first time I was in a cab going over the Brooklyn Bridge after a particularly strenuous night of naive and irresponsible tequila-pounding when I felt that unmistakable wave of vertigo and bile. I quickly realized two things: throw-up was imminent and there was no way we could pull over. Somehow, even through the acrid fog of my inebriation, I decided that the only way to preserve (a) my hardworking driver's leather interior and (b) a single shred of dignity was to calmly remove my wallet and keys from my purse and then discreetly puke inside of it.

The second incident took place a few years later, on the subway after an evening of Jameson on the rocks and swimming in my underpants. Still wet and listing to one side, I boarded a packed downtown Q train at Times Square and got about two stops when I realized what was about to happen. My options were: to projectile vomit into the center of the car, thus realizing a lifelong nightmare of becoming the dreaded "sick passenger" who causes a service delay; to get off the train at the next stop and heave into a conveniently located garbage can; or, finally, to use my imitation Marc Jacobs satchel as an emergency trash bag.

At the time, I really thought that, despite the fluorescent lighting and dozens of other people watching, no one could tell I was vomiting and not just rooting around in my purse for my keys with my entire face. I rode for another twenty minutes clutching my bag of throw-up with a smug smile, and then breezily tossed it into the garbage as I skipped home, as if to say, *Take that, world! I am a strong, independent woman who can have her cake and regurgitate it into her accessories, too!*

Despite the opinion of me you may be forming based on the above paragraphs, I came late to controlled substances. My idea of a crazy Saturday night in high school was to crack open a family-size bag of Starbursts and watch a bad bootleg videotape of the Broadway musical *Into the Woods* while applying a stinging layer of Jolen cream bleach to my upper lip. I don't remember ever even wanting to drink, although I did eye the kids who hung out under the archway at school, smoking cigarettes and sipping from bottles encased in paper bags, with a certain amount of envy. Mainly I just wanted to be noticed.

I had always sort of floated along, not cool enough to be embraced by the popular crowd nor pitiful enough to be singled out for their mockery, apart from occasional unibrow jokes. Social invisibility wasn't necessarily bad, but it did give me false hope that if I changed just a little, I could improve my status. This belief led to a number of identity crises, which were confusing both for me and everyone else in my life. In ninth grade, I wore baby barrettes and Doc Martens and traded in my Madonna and Whitney Houston tapes for Ani DiFranco and Liz Phair. In tenth grade, I wore sweatshirts and baggy jeans and became the manager of the varsity women's basketball team, a title that for some reason I thought came with street cred. In eleventh grade, I caked on Cover Girl foundation, spent all my Christmas money on clothes from the Limited, and got a modified version of the Rachel from my dad's tattooed barber. Still, I never got invited to the parties that I knew took place in apartments abandoned by trusting parents every weekend. I'm sure if I had been included, I would have just planted myself by a bowl of broken Fritos and smiled nervously off into the middle distance. But it would have been an honor just to have been nominated.

My breakthrough occurred on the last night of high school, at our graduation after-party, where everyone snuck off into Riverside Park to drink copious amounts of liquor, and eventually people got drunk enough to offer some to me. I was handed a can of Coke and a giant handle of Bacardi and, knowing absolutely nothing about drinking, I mixed them roughly half and half.

The world got slow and sparkly. I felt weightless. At one point, I skipped down Broadway arm in arm with two guys on another liquor run and leaned against the sweaty glass with my forehead while they got more beer. Then we were back under cover of trees, and I was sitting on the wall that separates the park from the sidewalk, laughing, laughing, and then, suddenly, puking all over myself.

I decamped to a bench, where I lay facedown and vomited through the cool wooden slats. At some point, someone threw water on me. Then they called an ambulance. I had to step over some other passed-out people to get to the curb, and that sobered me up right away. Suddenly I was belligerent. When I got to the hospital, I recited my social security number to the intake nurse and fixed her with a sloppy glare. She threw me in a cold shower and then discharged me into the care of my best friend, Anna, who was only slightly less drunk.

"Everyone is so worried about you," she slurred as we stumbled into a cab back to her house, where I had already been planning to spend the night.

"Like who?" I asked, my stomach turning over again as the driver shot out into traffic.

"Like, *everyone*," Anna said. "They can't believe it. It's all anyone is talking about."

I lay back against the seat, my damp hair sticking to my cheeks, my mouth still tasting like battery acid, and thought, *Finally. I've made it.*

⌒

That was my one and only flirtation with alcohol poisoning, and I do not recommend it as a means to social climbing. Now that I've learned how to do it in moderation, I enjoy drinking, and the occasional toke on a joint, which generally leads to the consumption of an entire bag of chips and two hours' worth of old *Sesame Street* clips on YouTube. But the path to responsible self-poisoning* has not been graceful.

For example, one bucolic afternoon during the fall of my freshman year of college, my friends Charlie and Carolyn and I decided to drive out to a movie theater in a suburban Connecticut town to see *Little Voice*, a British musical dramedy starring Michael Caine and Ewan McGregor. It was a Friday and we were eighteen, which seemed to us as good a reason as any to get drunk. Carolyn wisely

---

*Now that I read the words out loud, it doesn't actually seem that responsible. But apparently teetotalers have shorter life spans, so my hands are tied.

abstained, but Charlie and I mixed up a truly vomitous concoction we called "the Grasshopper." It consisted of Dubra vodka (which cost only seven dollars for a giant plastic jug), Mountain Dew, and cherry Kool-Aid. We poured the mixture back into the soda bottles and smuggled them into the theater.

According to IMDb, *Little Voice* is the story of a shy, reclusive woman who spends her downtime listening to old records and belting out Judy Garland hits to her dead father's ghost. I had to look this up because I remember literally nothing about the movie except for the fact that, at some point, something catches on fire. This detail sticks with me because it prompted me to burst into hysterical sobs. The Mountain Dew bottles were twenty ounces, the cocktail tasted like Hawaiian Punch, and so I chugged it like it was a soda. As I wept, Charlie and Carolyn ushered me out of the theater and drove me home, and to thank them I threw up the vile red menace all over the backseat of Charlie's Toyota Land Cruiser. (I was not carrying a purse at the time.)

Like every other college freshman, as part of my orientation I memorized the singsong rhyme that has guided many an amateur drinker through their first fratty weeks of hedonism:

Beer before liquor, never sicker;
Liquor before beer, you're in the clear.

I don't really drink beer, so I've never been able to put this mantra to the test. However, I suspect that it's fallible based on the fact that it makes no stipulations as to the quantity of either beer or liquor consumed. For instance, will one Michelob Light followed by a vodka cranberry really wreak more havoc than three shots of grain alcohol chased with a case of Guinness? College kids take rules literally, and we need to come up with more specific guidelines if we want to keep them safe. Here, based on my years of experience, are a few alternative rhymes:

Cilantro-sage-infused cocktail
Marks the bartender's betrayal.

Tequila shooters seem so naughty
'Til you're hunched over the potty.

Five bottles for four friends: This math
Leads you straight down Satan's path.

Milk is healthful and nutritious
But pairing it with booze is injudicious.

Lonely drinking gone awry:
Sob while eating week-old Thai.

Each of these lessons was gleaned in the decade between twenty and thirty, as I checked one boozy rite of passage after another off my list: first legal drink; first refusal of well liquor out of self-respect; first dinner party thrown with wine not made by Carlo Rossi; first time getting into a bar without ID based solely on crow's-feet; first regression back to binge-drinking Jose Cuervo based on bouncer's comments about crow's-feet . . . everyone's is personal to some extent, but you can count on a slow but steady increase in the quality of the alcohol you drink, coupled with a change of location. One minute you're shouting over the din to fifteen friends in a packed bar on a Friday; the next, you're settling in for a Tuesday night of DVR with you, yourself, and a fishbowl-size glass of wine. Which, for me, was the sweet spot I had been searching for ever since my face hit that bench in Riverside Park. I was never cut out for serious drinking. Wine and cheese is much more my speed. And slippers. And a humidifier. And expensive eye cream, because that bouncer still haunts my dreams.

As I entered my thirties, I felt good about my drinking. I always had a decent bottle of red in the pantry, a husband to share it with, and friends with a similar distaste for trance music and being humped by strangers. Me and my liver, it seemed like we had our whole lives ahead of us.

And then I got pregnant.

⌒

Long before I became a mother, I was, as my Sonoma County aunt is fond of saying, "a lover of the grape." When I learned of my fecundity, I panicked, and not for the normal reasons, like the fear that all women have upon conception that they will end up looking like a fully inflated Violet Beauregarde until the end of time. No, I worried that I wouldn't be able to keep the baby a secret. Not drinking would be a dead giveaway to my friends, so I continued to hold stemware at parties, feigning sips, because to abstain among anyone who had seen the old, half-a-bottle-a-night me in action, the jig would immediately be up.

My pregnancy, of course, was mostly booze-free. I thought this would be an ordeal, with some kind of terrifying, *Trainspotting*-esque withdrawal sequence in which I sweated and keened and tried to carve my way into a box of wine with a Bic pen. Both my general practitioner and my midwife assured me that the occasional drink—even a few ounces of wine every day!—would be fine, but surprisingly I found that my cravings for egg salad sandwiches and watermelon eclipsed my nostalgia for riojas and tempranillos. I harbored abstinence-induced fantasies of glugging a delicious, fat glass of red as soon as I went into labor, for relaxation and pain-killing purposes, but since it ended up starting at six a.m., the first contractions promptly followed by retching over the side of the bed into a Citarella bag, I did not, in the end, feel like a drink.

That all changed by the time my son was about two months old. Once I had adjusted to the constant sleep deprivation and completed the Mensa application that is the unassisted donning of a Moby Wrap, I felt ready to take a happy hour test run.

I started with an adventurous outing—by which I mean something that involved pants with a button, washing my hair, and taking the subway: meeting a friend, who in my former life had been a favorite drinking buddy, at a downtown bar at five p.m. I ordered a glass of wine and single-handedly demolished a bowl of complimentary potato chips with the vacuum power (and approximate grace) of a Flowbee. Nothing abnormal there. But as the dinner rush started and people filled the bar, I received some lingering glances. Because on my lap, buried under the potato detritus, sat my kid. He was relatively quiet, especially given the noise, but seemed out of place attempting to gnaw on the craft beer taps. My friend was proud of me, and even bragged on Facebook that she'd lured Sam out to his first bar. But I was self-conscious.

"People *judged* me," I reported to my husband when I got home, still pleasantly relaxed from my drink, which was prominently displayed on my leg from when Sam had grabbed at the stem, sending precious droplets sloshing.

"I'm sure they weren't judging you."

"No, they *did*," I insisted. "It was like that line, from *Sweet Home Alabama*."

He blinked. "You'll have to refresh my memory."

" 'You have a *baby* . . . in a *bar*,' " I said, approximating Reese Witherspoon's Tennessee twang. Jeff furrowed his brow.

"Well, I mean . . . you did."

"You're missing the nuance of the delivery!" I shouted, and I stormed off to get back into my maternity jeggings.

A few weeks later, I learned that a German beer hall in my neighborhood hosted weekly "playdates" in the midafternoon, before patrons employed by larger and presumably more continent bosses got out of work. I showed up at two thirty on a Thursday to find colorful mats covering the floors and fellow nursing moms nursing liters of pale beer cross-legged as their infants flailed beneath them.

The atmosphere seemed friendly enough, until a sour-faced twentysomething bartender approached and had me sign a sobering waiver promising never to let my child touch anything outside the boundary of the play space and swear upon pain of expulsion to use the changing table—inexplicably located in the men's room—for diaper duty. I got that it was health code stuff, but the contract still seemed awfully formal. That, coupled with the fact that there were no drink specials, left me cold. So I turned to my last resort: playgroup.

Every week or so I was meeting with a small klatch of other moms and their babies at one of our Brooklyn homes. E-mails were usually exchanged the day before to plan the potluck menu.

I'm picking up some hummus and carrot sticks! one would write.

I'm trying some no-bake energy balls I saw on Pinterest! another might chime in.

One week, the host was going through a personal crisis, so I jumped at the opportunity to drown her sorrows. *If only you were a drinker, I would bring a bottle of wine for "snack,"* I typed, adding a winking emoticon to communicate that I was totally kidding, ha-ha, unless . . . she was into it.

I hit send.

Seconds later, a reply came from one of the other members: *So glad you said it—I've been dying to suggest a little boozy playgroup but didn't want to sound like the alchy mom!!*

That Wednesday we cheered impishly as we popped a bottle of Prosecco. If David Attenborough had been narrating the scene, he might have observed, *The American stay-at-home mother, unable to keep social engagements after five p.m. with any reliability and shamed out of bringing a stroller to the local cocktail bar, finds comfort in tippling away during daylight hours with others of her species.* In my prebaby life, daytime drinking might have signaled a problem; now, it seemed the only acceptable time. *Oh, well,* I thought, tipping back my glass as Raffi recited the colors *en español*. *When in Rome!* Which was the most depressing thing I could have said, since Rome has the Coliseum and the Sistine Chapel and spaghetti carbonara, and I was sitting on a urineproof plastic pad, wet spots blooming on my T-shirt as I ate peanut butter mixed with oats in sticky globs the size of horse testicles.

Eventually, that playgroup disbanded and I reverted to my pre-baby drinking ritual, which involves zero travel and one hundred percent more television, math I can really get behind. Now most nights after Sam falls asleep I have a glass of wine while very quietly watching *Masters of Sex* on my computer, with headphones. It's a party, I'm not gonna lie. And when I feel that tug of doubt that shadows pretty much every moment of motherhood but especially the self-indulgent ones, the voice that wonders aloud in my ear if maybe I'm not being a little *irresponsible*, and that maybe instead of illegally streaming explicit Showtime dramas and getting tipsy I should be fermenting my own Play-Doh or learning how to make a pancake that doesn't look like the Elephant Man, I tell it to hush.

Because I am a grown woman who has learned how to hold her drink, and care for her child, who has a closet floor full of unsullied purses—unless you count dried banana—and a glass that is metaphorically, and also hopefully literally, half-full. At least most of the time.

Gratuitous Foodity

Lately I've noticed a troubling trend. Whenever I ask my husband to fetch or prepare food for me I have to give him orders that make me sound like a disgusting, down-market version of Meg Ryan in *When Harry Met Sally*.

On coffee

"Put in *a lot* of half-and-half, okay? More than you think anyone would want. Try to achieve a cup of half-and-half with a subtle coffee flavor. And don't skimp on the sugar. Give me four packets, and if they only have the big pour containers, turn it upside down and count to ten, and make sure no lumps are obstructing the opening."

On sandwiches

"I want more mayonnaise than the FDA advises a single person to consume at one sitting. Put on an amount that makes you recoil and then add another teaspoon. Also I want the cheese layer to be thicker than the meat layer by a ratio of two to one."

On fries

"It should look like you're making a *Carrie* diorama, only the people are fries and the blood is ketchup. I want the splatter to reach all four corners of the container. They should need to call in Dexter."

⌒

The hard truth is that I can get away with being a truly revolting eater because I'm thin. It's not fair, but it's a fact: if you're a small person, you can shove all manner of junk in your face and people will titter and say, "Oh, where does it *go*?" like you're adorable for trying to eat a whole ham in one sitting. For some reason our culture has decided that a thin person eating a six-foot sub is cute, while a heavy person doing the same thing is a slob and should be fat-shamed until he or she learns to live on steamed salmon and wilted spinach seasoned only with his or her own bitter tears. So I have made it my mission in life to disgust people with my food choices, until they are forced to persecute me, too.

⌒

I saw a tweet from *The Tyra Banks Show* the other day that asked, *Do you folks have any "BFF's: Best Food Frenemies"?!*

Oh, sweet fancy cupcakes, *yes*, I thought, smizing with my epiglottis.

First of all, since you asked, Tyra: nachos. With everything. Suspect-looking ground beef, black beans, gobs of sour cream and guac, melted cheese, jalapeños . . . I like the chips to take on a mushy, wilted consistency so that I can eat my nachos with a spoon.

Next, Tater Tots. Crispy and golden brown, drowning in ketchup. I used to be so jealous when the school lunch included Tater Tots and I was stuck with my sad whole-wheat peanut butter (no jelly) sandwich that no one wanted to trade for.

Frosted strawberry Pop-Tarts, toasted to slightly burned ooziness, served with a tall glass of cold whole milk.

Rice Krispies Treats. Not the kind they sell at bodegas; the kind you make from scratch that taste like real butter and stick to your fingers. I can't make these anymore because I just start eating from the pan before they cool and then I get a crazy sugar high and start reorganizing my closet.

Pasta. I love pasta so fucking much I'd be the Mario Batali of loving pasta if Mario Batali didn't already exist. If I had to cut out carbs I would want to kill myself, and I would do it *with pasta*. Giant bowls of linguine with fresh clam sauce, tortellini with pesto and Parmesan cheese, penne à la vodka, orecchiette with sausage and cream, spaghetti carbonara, baked ziti, rigatoni Bolognese, oozing lasagnas . . . I'm actually aroused right now. Tell the Papa John's delivery boy to *stay in the car*.

Indian food, specifically rich, creamy chicken tikka masala (in keeping with my fat-laden palate, I like only developing-world food designed for American food courts) into which I dip chunks of soft, warm naan. Rice? Fuck the bowl of rice. (Sorry, Asia.)

Sushi, especially spicy salmon rolls liberally topped with that heavenly spicy mayonnaise that negates the healthfulness of the fish. (Sorry again, Asia; Japan this time.)

Everything bagels, the perfect crispy-on-the-outside, chewy-on-the-inside New York kind, slathered with full-fat cream cheese and topped with a thin slice of lox.

An artery-clogging cheese plate—triple-crème L'Explorateur, creamy goat cheese with truffles, nutty Manchego, smoked Gouda, and extra-sharp cheddar—served with slices of crusty French bread.

Oh, whoops. I just clicked on the *Tyra Show*'s link and they meant friends who tempt you to eat more, not frenemies actually made of food.

Whatever, Tyra. Me and Nachos don't need you anyway.

Ten Fictional Restaurants I Fantasize About Eating at Probably More Than Is Normal

10. Captain Hook Fish and Chips, in *Fast Times at Ridgemont High*

I don't even really like fish, but Judge Reinhold dressed as a pirate seals the deal.

9. The Max, in *Saved by the Bell*

Not so much for the menu; more for the subtly elegant neon geometric '80s decor and impromptu dance performances.

8. Chotchkie's, in *Office Space*

Because I like finding pieces of flair in my food.

7. McDowell's, in *Coming to America*

When even the janitor is wearing a plaid bow tie, you know you're in for some fine-ass dining.

6. T.G.I. Friday's . . . but only the one from *Cocktail*, where Tom Cruise throws drinks in the air

(Get Donald Glover to make quesadillas while twerking at Applebee's and I *might* reconsider.)

5. Jackrabbit Slim's, in *Pulp Fiction*

A boring choice, maybe, but who can resist eating in a *car*? (And no, McDonald's in the backseat of our family's 1979 Datsun trapped in 1-95 traffic does not count.) Also, in today's economy that much-maligned five-dollar shake seems like a deal.

4. The Peach Pit, in *Beverly Hills, 90210*

Because I would like fries with Brandon Walsh's dreamy eyes and white-boy flattop.

3. The Lanford Lunch Box, in *Roseanne*

What does it say about me that I'm basically *dying* to be served a sloppy joe by Roseanne? Is this as obviously sexual as the dream I had in eighth grade about sitting on a plane next to David Duchovny?

2. Ziggy's Ice Cream Parlor, in *Bill & Ted's Excellent Adventure*

I'm 99 percent positive I could finish the "Ziggy Pig" but there's only one way to find out. And it's killing me a little bit inside that I can't.

1. The Italian restaurant in *Defending Your Life*

Anyone who's seen this 1991 Albert Brooks gem knows that when you're hanging out between life and afterlife, calories don't exist. The conceit of the running gag is that you can eat as much as you want of the most delicious food you've ever tasted and you'll never feel sick or gain weight. So, yeah. That's the holy grail of totally made-up eateries where I would face-plant into the hot buffet in my appetite-whetting dreams.

I feel like this list was a really good use of our collective time, don't you?

RECIPE SECTION

(This was important to include so that the book cover can feature the words "Recipes Inside!" This is my second-favorite food-related advertising phrase, after "Pudding in the Mix!" and I think it will help sales if this ever ends up shoved next to the stack of *Prevention* magazines by the checkout at Super Stop & Shop.)

Sacri*licious* Expired Easter Cake

Directions

1. Buy frozen Sara Lee pound cake. Serve with whipped cream and strawberries, then return to fridge in questionably loose Saran wrapping.

2. Approximately two weeks later, gingerly lift bricklike remains of cake from aluminum container. Arrange in center of plate.

3. Using expired whipped cream, make a mound in the center of the cake and two football-shaped ears at the top.

4. Find raisins. There are always raisins somewhere—check your carpets and the bottom of all your (non-vomited-in) purses. Use smidges of whipped cream to affix raisins in and above center mound in approximation of eyes and nose.

5. Before you put it away, dispense whipped cream directly into mouth. (Whipped cream never *really* goes bad, plus at least you're not doing something more dangerous, like whippets.)

6. Did you bake a cake in the last three years? Then surely you have some dusty tubes of congealed icing somewhere in the pantry! Drag those suckers out, and use to make nose, eyebrows (optional), mouth, and inner ear.

7. Use icing to write tender Easter message to Jesus (alternative idea: "What's up, Doc?").

8. Present to horrified Catholic relatives.

Serving suggestions: Actually, you probably should not eat this.

Tootsie Roll Log Cabin

Where Satan lives, obviously.

Directions

1. Take giant bowl of Tootsie Rolls, unwrap while watching premiere of *The Real Housewives of Wherever* and drinking wine.

2. Stack them haphazardly, like Pa Ingalls might have done, if he had also been drunk. Drink more wine.

3. Attempt to stick Twizzler roof on with honey. Realize this is a bad idea. Drink more wine, and fetch sewing kit you have never used for anything other than attempting to fasten Twizzler roof to Tootsie Roll log cabin—Mom *did* always say it would come in handy!

4. Pin Twizzlers to cabin. Present to husband. Beam when he asks, "Is it a . . . turd yurt?"

5. Eat, as you are compelled to do with all failed arts and crafts projects. Dodge pins to avoid tongue piercing.

One of my favorite varieties of news stories is People Getting into (Nonfatal) Physical Fights over Trivial Things. My favorite *sub-*

category of that oeuvre is People Getting into (Nonfatal) Physical Fights over Food. And if I had to choose a favorite *sub*-subcategory, it would have to be People Getting into (Nonfatal) Physical Fights over Food That Costs Less than Four Dollars.

Lucky for me, there are literally countless instances of this phenomenon in America, also known as VH1's Most Awesomely Baddest Country on Earth, and hungry tempers seem to flare most frequently in the winter. They should rename February Don't Touch My Food, Bitch month. (I'm sure Black History will understand.)

While perusing news on the subject, the biggest lesson seems to be: do not frequent fast-food drive-throughs after dark, especially in Waco, Texas, or anywhere in Massachusetts. But I'm more interested in the intimate battles set in private homes, in which one person steals from another person's private stash. For example, the case in Staten Island a few years ago in which a sixteen-year-old kidnapped her boyfriend's daughter after he smacked her . . . for eating the last Hot Pocket. Yes, that's a class B felony with a sentence of one to three years in prison . . . in the name of Hot Pockets. If I ever run for office and Sean Hannity asks me on national TV why I love America, that is the story I'm going to tell.

But I think my all-time favorite Physical Fight over Food That Costs Less than Four Dollars was when a Florida woman threatened her roommate with scissors, hit her with a *board*, and then knocked her to the ground and beat her because the roommate had fed a box of her Thin Mints . . . to the assailant's own hungry children.

Now, the Hot Pocket incident just seems silly to me, since that dude could easily have just gone to the nearest 7-Eleven. But Girl Scout cookies . . . those are precious. In the off season, you'd have an easier time buying crack than getting your hands on a box of Samoas.

That's not a joke, by the way, it's a fact.

ONE OF THESE THINGS IS NOT LIKE THE OTHER:
A HIGHLY SUSPICIOUS COMPARATIVE ANALYSIS

	POT	HOOKER	CRACK	BOOZE	GIRL SCOUT COOKIES
Have to "know a guy"	✓	✓	✓		✓
Cash only	✓	✓	✓		✓
Can order online		✓		✓	☹
ILLEGAL	✓	✓	✓	✓ (under 21)	WTF?

Seriously, why are Girl Scout cookies harder to procure than illegal drugs? There is something wrong with that lesson. If I sent you on a scavenger hunt right now with a list that included a quart of unpasteurized raw milk, an ounce of marijuana, an eight-ball of cocaine, a whole roasted goat, and a box of Thin Mints, guess which item would be the biggest bitch to find? That is *not right*.

The main reason for this, of course, is that Girl Scouts are forbidden from selling cookies online. I'm not really sure why this is—I can only guess it's to even the playing field and avoid excessive gaming of the system—but it seems pretty archaic. Explain to me, how is forcing preteens in short, pleated skirts to walk the streets soliciting strangers character building? If you go to the Girl Scouts of America website, they explain they don't currently allow online sales, but that you can "use the Find Cookies! search box to help you find Girl Scouts selling cookies." Yes, that's right. Anyone can log onto this website to locate young girls anywhere in the country, and yet I cannot get my Tagalong fix using Amazon Prime shipping.

The yearly experience of trolling for cookies makes me feel like a creep. I find myself breathlessly tweeting sentences that are probably on government Megan's Law watch lists: *Anyone know any Girl Scouts? I NEED one. Anywhere in the country. I'll pay anything!!!!* I stare a little too long at kids on the street, searching their outfits for telltale flashes of green. They're the world's tiniest drug dealers and, as with real drugs, I am not cool enough to have a reliable hookup.

I'm just going to have to keep having kids until I get a daughter and can force her into the trade. Maybe I'll even name her Peanut Butter Patty, for incentive. Or, if she's bland and homely, Trefoil. But at this point, who am I kidding, I'll take what I can get.

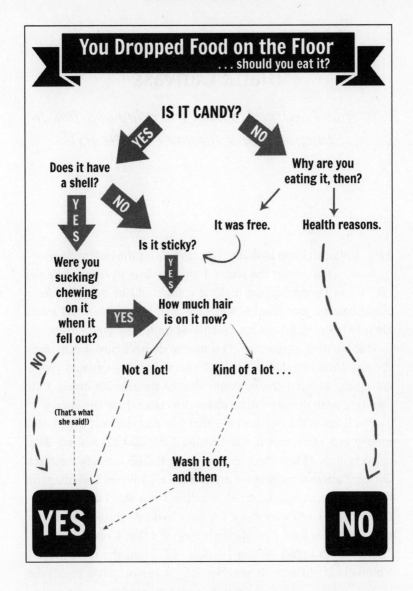

You Dropped Food on the Floor
. . . should you eat it?

IS IT CANDY?

YES — Does it have a shell?

NO — Why are you eating it, then?

Does it have a shell?
- YES → Were you sucking/chewing on it when it fell out?
  - NO / (That's what she said!) → YES
- NO → Is it sticky?

Is it sticky?
- YES → How much hair is on it now?
  - YES → How much hair is on it now?

Why are you eating it, then?
- It was free.
- Health reasons.

How much hair is on it now?
- Not a lot! → YES
- Kind of a lot . . . → Wash it off, and then → YES

It was free. → Is it sticky?

Health reasons. → NO

YES

NO

Blank Canvass

Or, How I Learned to Stop Worrying and Talk to Strangers (for a Total of Four Hours)

"Hello, sir! You look like you care about the environment!"
Let me set the scene: I am standing in front of Babies "R" Us in Union Square, making what could be mistaken for a single, spastic jazz hand at a middle-aged man fifteen feet away. He rolls his eyes, takes a drag on his cigarette, and pointedly tosses it, still burning, at my feet. Perhaps he doesn't care much about the environment after all. It is a beautiful spring day and people are trying to enjoy the sunshine during their lunch break. I am standing in their way. I am a street canvasser. I am the enemy.

I've lived in the city for my entire life, and the only time I gave money to a canvasser it was because I thought he was my Thai deliveryman. (Memo to the New York Public Interest Research Group: I am still waiting for my pad see ew.) When I see them on the street I pick up a fake phone call. It's not that I don't support their causes (well, except for the poor bastards shilling for salons who ask me where I get my hair cut); it's that I hate, hate, *hate* talking to strangers. When I was a kid, I had the most passive lemonade stand ever. It was basically a performance piece: me, sitting silently on my stoop with a sweaty pitcher, terror etched on my face, praying for people to heed the words of Dionne Warwick and walk on by.

Friends who grew up in the suburbs and who are thinking about having kids often ask me about the drawbacks of being a city child, and really the only one I can come up with is the learned misanthropy. Part of this is definitely specific to my father's side of the family. We vacationed every summer on tiny Block Island, not quite ten square miles in size, for twenty-five years and my dad never made a single friend, a record I deeply respect. Also, my grandmother, after learning that one of her neighbors at the retirement home where she lives had reported her smoking to the management, chased the poor woman down the hallway, shouting, "You'd better run, bitch!" So maybe New York is not entirely to blame.

Still, it's hard not to grow to hate strangers when you live in a crush of so many. There are *so* many people pushing and bumping and crowding you at all times that they can sometimes amass into one anonymous blob that you just try to tune out as a whole. Often, as an adult, I'll find myself sitting on the subway and realize that I don't look at my fellow riders as real people but more like loud, annoyingly placed props. And yes, I understand this makes me sound like a sociopath, but try riding the New York transit system on a daily basis and see if you don't start to turn a little dark. It's just part of the deal of living here, like accepting that you can never wear white jeans or find parking. On the plus side, we have *great* bagels.

I generally avoid contact with strangers in any geographic location at all costs, but if I had to choose my two *least* favorite kinds of strangers to encounter (not including the obviously mentally ill, which weeds out a *lot* of New Yorkers) I would pick: People Who Obliviously Stand in Your Way and People Who Try to Sell You Things on the Street.

PWOSIYW are, at best, confused tourists and, at worst, d-bags who don't budge from what is apparently their permanent home address aggressively leaning against the subway doors, even when said doors open onto a packed platform. PWTTSYTOTS almost always deserve your sympathy (person in costume handing out flyers for going-out-of-business electronics store; Scientologists hawking *Dianetics*) but almost never deserve your money. (The only exception to this rule is in the case of mobile food carts. Sell me any kind of food out of a steaming vat of questionable cleanliness and I will eat it. In fact, I will take two.) And then there is the dreaded canvasser, who wins the title of my least, least, least favorite stranger of all time. Being people who *purposefully* stand in your way *while* they try to sell you things, they are more powerful, wily, and annoying than each previously mentioned species could ever be alone. And they are *everywhere*.

On an ethical level, I realize, street canvassers are hard to hate. They stand outside all day trying to raise money for charitable organizations with admirable mission statements or for scrappy, underdog political candidates they'd willingly follow off a cliff or into a sex dungeon. But I still hate them. And then, in the guise of a shamefully self-promoting stunt, I became one.

I was trying to expand my writing portfolio at the time and had met the new editor of a weekly tabloid newspaper at a party. He suggested I pitch him some story ideas for a first-person account of some quirky New York experience. *I'll join the Rockettes for a day!* I thought gleefully. *I'll try out for the roller derby!* But then, almost as an aside, I tacked on one last idea:

> I personally loathe street lobbyists. They make me uncomfortable; they ask me about my hair, then try to shame me into taking a moment for something I actually support, like gay rights. I think most NYers feel the way I do, so it would be fun (well, not *fun*, as I would want to kill myself) to shadow and/or become one and write about the experience.

It was my own fault, and so I tried to approach the assignment as character building. I would be facing my fear—sort of like what I did multiple times a day when I peered into the toilet bowl looking for rats. And maybe, just maybe, it would help me to humanize the poor saps I normally passed without so much as a side-eye.

It took a few phone calls and e-mails, but within a week I had convinced the ACLU—my dad is a former employee and board member, so I jacked open that door using nepotism like a crowbar!—and Greenpeace to let me tag along with them for one afternoon. *One.* I insisted that brevity was key, knowing that I would never come back for a second day, even if I promised to, and I spent the week prior to my mission in the Dominican Republic with a group of friends, sucking down rum and Cokes in an attempt to quell my growing sense of unease. My fear was so out of control that I actually considered faking it at one point, just standing outside my apartment building pretending to be a canvasser.

"I'm sure I can get the gist in a few minutes, right?" I asked my husband.

"Hey," he said, "it worked for Jayson Blair."

My first gig was with the ACLU, and I arrived at the streamer-festooned office in Herald Square trying hard not to cry.

David, the lanky and charismatic regional canvassing director, greeted me at the door and ushered me in to meet his team, a band of fresh-scrubbed twentysomethings, at least three of whom seemed to be named Alex. They seemed suspiciously devoid of any signs that they, too, might have downed an entire bottle of tempranillo the previous night while catching up on *Sixteen and Pregnant*. I felt immediately at a disadvantage.

A woman named Amanda, with blue eyes, blond ringlets, and a cheery camp counselor disposition, was given the task of training me. Amanda told me she'd been canvassing for various organizations since 2007, and when I asked, sincerely, why she did it, she practically beamed. "It's *so* fun! And rewarding!" I asked if

New York was the toughest city she had canvassed and she shook her head. "New Yorkers are very socially conscious," she said brightly, and then, her eyebrows crinkling in a thrilling flash of pain, she added, "It's getting them to *stop* that's hard." I wanted to press her on whether constantly being ignored or sneered at had any effect on her drinking habits or prescription medications, but as I was trying to formulate a non-judgy-sounding question she moved on. "My biggest tip is to maintain a perma-grin," she confided. "People are like babies; if you smile at them, they'll smile." I smiled; she smiled. Then she gave me my "rap" to memorize. (It's too bad real rap wouldn't have helped, because I know all the lyrics to "The Humpty Dance." Talking to strangers on the street in broad daylight? Pass. Make a fool of myself in front of strangers at a karaoke bar? Don't mind if I do!) Nearby, the group of Alexes was working on what they called "positive leaves," otherwise known as telling people to have a good day even if they are flipping you off.

I was hoping that Amanda and David might just let me shadow them, but no—when we arrived at our Lincoln Center location, I was given an extra-large blue ACLU vest, which gave me the appearance of a portly, progressive Smurf. Before we started on real people, we practiced "grabbing" each other (again, sadly not literal; "making a grab" means stopping someone), and then one of the Alexes gave me a pep talk.

"I want you to make six stops before lunch and raise two hundred dollars," he said.

"Couldn't I have more modest goals?" I asked. "Like 'Don't vomit on yourself' or 'Try not to say "fuck"'?" Alex laughed and held up his fist. I had no choice but to bump it.

I assumed my position, stationed next to Amanda and facing David, thirty feet away, thus forming a triangle designed to trap almost everyone who tried to avoid us.

"Hello there!" I called unconvincingly to passersby. "Do you have a moment for gay rights?" I was barely even looking at the people I was talking to, regressing to my tried-and-true total avoidance sales tactics, but still, within five minutes I got a stop. The man, a Kris Kringle doppelgänger, slowed as he approached.

"I think *I* have the civil right to walk down the street without being ambushed!" he said angrily, his face growing red.

I know, right? I wanted to shout, but instead I just chirped, "Thanks," smiling so hard my cheeks hurt.

"You get one of those every so often," Amanda said once Santa had stomped out of earshot. "But most people are nice." Turned out, she was right—to my surprise, I was not verbally abused again for the remainder of my shift, and I got to observe some interesting patterns. People generally fell into one of three categories: they ignored me completely, politely declined (my personal favorite demurrals—"Not today" or "I'm good"—both suggested that the person in question had recently overindulged in gay rights), or stopped because they didn't speak English well enough to know what I was saying. I performed my "rap" for at least a half dozen kindly, confused foreigners. Amanda insisted that statistically, one out of every five people who stop make a donation, but at the end of two hours I had ten stops and nothing to show for it, like I'd been unsuccessfully speed dating with all of New York. David and Amanda, meanwhile, seemed to convince people effortlessly to hand over their credit cards. I don't know what bothered me more, standing in the West Sixties dressed in my Smurf village best and soliciting money, or the fact that I sucked at it so much.

I set out to improve my track record during my second outing a few days later. This time I was with Greenpeace, and whereas the ACLU trained me for less than an hour before sending me out, Greenpeace made me attend a day-long orientation.

Its office in Williamsburg was unmarked but for a series of stickers on the street entrance; upstairs, the office door bore a sign reading "Welcome to the Revolution." I had to command my eyes not to roll out of their sockets. Amy, one of the New York City coordinators, who had a bored, suspicious demeanor that I immediately respected, introduced me to four other novice canvassers and then sized me up while she took a cigarette break (American Spirits, like you even had to ask). As she spoke, revealing a sardonic sense of humor, I realized that if the ACLU was camp counselors, then Greenpeace was the camper sneaking peyote in the woods. When I asked if there would be a rap to memorize, Amy snorted at the outdated word and then smiled. "We're not *robots*," she said.

My training began with an overview of Greenpeace's history and mission, which included a YouTube video in which a man opened a Kit Kat bar to reveal an orangutan finger, which he then proceeded to eat, blood streaming down his face. This ad was meant to put pressure on Nestlé to stop buying palm oil produced by deforestation in Indonesia. I was later relieved to learn that the United States is the only country in which Kit Kats are produced under license by Hershey, which makes biting down on a dismembered digit far less likely.

Amy walked us through the basics of canvassing, mapping out the lesson on a wall-size chalkboard. Unlike the ACLU, Greenpeace discouraged its canvassers from using yes or no questions as opening lines. Amy suggested something more impassioned ("Let's fight global warming today!") or assumptive ("I know *you* care about whales!"). Apparently one Greenpeace staffer, who went by the code name "Crawdaddy," liked to open with the zinger, "What does a burning orangutan smell like?"

Once we got someone to stop, using either Crawdaddy's method or something less fucking insane, our job was to outline a specific problem, the solution, and past Greenpeace victories that would make potential members want to give us money. Amy asked us to choose either deforestation or whaling for our pitch, and since the two people before me chose deforestation, I chose whales just to be different. I also choose wine based on the label. That's just the seat-of-the-pants lifestyle I lead.

Despite having already lost my canvassing virginity, I was nervous the following morning as I arrived in Union Square with Amy and the Greenpeace team. We huddled on the steps at Fourteenth Street, put on baby blue T-shirts, and got our assignments. I was dispatched to the Babies "R" Us with two seasoned staffers, Matthias and Ben, big, handsome guys who comfortably used their charm as a hook. "What are you texting about, trees?" Matthias called to a woman standing at a bus stop, absorbed in her BlackBerry. She looked up, smiled, and blushed. His battle was half-won.

I was failing miserably. Again. After a few attempts, I couldn't bring myself to tell one more person that they looked like they loved whales, so I reverted to the forbidden yes or no questions. I tried flirting, and a few men stopped for me, their eyes glazing over as I began eagerly educating them about the lifting of a commercial whaling ban, but I couldn't close a single deal. "You have to believe they're going to sign up," Ben told me. "They can see it in your eyes if you don't."

"Can I wear sunglasses?" I asked hopefully.

"No," he barked, and went back to work. "Clean, renewable energy!" he bellowed to anyone in earshot. "Let's! Make! It! Happen!"

At the end of my shift I was shamefully empty-handed, and it is to their credit that the Greenpeacers were sympathetic. "A lot of people don't come back after their first day," Ben said earnestly. "It's a hard job, but if you love doing it, it's incredible." I felt like hugging him, but instead I took out my wallet, and as I dictated my credit card number, mentally calculating the dent that twenty dollars a month would make in my unsustainably farmed sushi budget, I knew in my heart of hearts that I was only doing it to make them like me. But I wanted to seem less selfish, so I tried to look at it differently. After all, I had canvassed for a few measly hours and couldn't hack it, while the people I'd met—and countless more—were on the streets every day with smiles on their faces and clipboards at the ready, trying to raise money for causes they believed in. The least I could give them to make up for ten years of fake phone calls was a small donation.

A few months later, I quietly canceled the credit card. I'm sure I could have called and ended my membership, but that would have involved voice-on-voice contact, and I just hate talking to people I don't know.

SHIT LIST BINGO

Close family friend who never gave you a wedding gift	Bus driver who identified you by the wrong gender during an experimental hair phase	Neighbor who left passive-aggressive note on your unsorted recycling	Your romantic partner, for whatever today's reason is	Man who unapologetically cut Trader Joe's line because he "only had this one thing"
Men who sit in shared public spaces like they need three feet just for their nuts	Former flame who hasn't followed you back on Twitter	Anyone with a better body	Obnoxious fictional character who failed to die at the end	Sallie Fucking Mae
Lady at yoga who gives you side-eye for no reason	Anyone with more money	★	Anyone less petty and spiteful	Lady at yoga YOU give side-eye to for no reason
Grade school classmate who called you a name in 1987	Designer whose clothes don't fit in what is your normal size everywhere else	Anyone with better hair	Celebrity whose career you have always felt you deserved . . . if you had any talent or ambition	Distant acquaintance who keeps inviting you to play FarmVille on Facebook
Cashier who asked if those two cupcakes were "both for you?"	Lotto bitch who never calls your numbers	Political pundit from across the aisle who is clearly a product of inbreeding	People who misplace apostrophe's like moron's	Anyone whose shit list you are on

I'm Not a Girl . . . Not Yet a Golden Girl

I started thinking about the portrayal of moms in pop culture, ironically, while watching an episode of *Girls*. Specifically, it was the first-season scene in which two of the series' (platonic, female) twentysomething protagonists bond by way of a shared bath. My first thought was, *I have never casually bathed with a friend while discussing my sex life.* My second was, *I would literally pay someone if they could guarantee me a bath that no one else would try to climb into.*

You see, I have a toddler. He is there when I bathe. He is there when I pee. He is always there, like another limb that just happens to move around independently of the rest of my body. And he has changed everything.

The twentysomething characters on *Girls* are gloriously, maddeningly self-involved. They fret over outfits, they dish about guys, they have kinky, acrobatic sex in all manner of shabby-chichi New York apartments. They also get naked in front of each other in many nonsexual situations (see above), as if to prove that nudity can reach a saturation point at which it ceases to matter. I love the show, despite its tendency to make me feel like I wasted my twenties eating toaster pizzas and watching *The Bachelorette*, and I have a hunch that Lena Dunham chose the title *Girls* precisely because it sounds so youthful and frivolous. They are point-edly *not* women. And they are definitely not moms.

I'm a thirtysomething mother who drinks (a lot of) wine, has (occasional, let's not get crazy here) sex, and (sometimes) wears low-rise jeans. I also sometimes choose sensible shoes, let my eye-brows get scraggly, and gripe at my husband for letting the dishes pile up. I'm reasonably happy, but I screw up a lot. I'm self-involved, but I can't afford to be that way all of the time anymore, because I devote so much of myself to someone much needier than I am. I feel like I'm pretty representational of my mom friends, a group largely composed of ambitious, creative, funny, and flawed upper-middle-class women. A mother in her early thirties with a committed partner and a child with no extraordinary or dramatic challenges doesn't seem like an endangered species, and yet I don't see us represented accurately anywhere on TV or in movies. The fictional character who comes closest to realism is probably Alyson Hannigan's Lily on *How I Met Your Mother*, but I disqual-ified her when, seemingly days after giving birth, her character started showing up at the bar again to hang with her friends every night. Sorry, but in real life moms don't get to do that. Instead, they drink alone while watching *How I Met Your Mother*.

Moms don't get a lot of choices when it comes to cultural rep-resentation. Yes, women of many ages, colors, and sizes show up on screens both big and small, dragging all manner of progeny in tow, but in a world with thousands of different candy bars at ev-ery truck stop and hundreds of unique brands of toilet paper, when it comes to the definition of mothers in our culture we seem able to come up with only two flavors: martyr and MILF. Both categories seem designed to strip women, regardless of their ab-dominal fitness levels or career choices, of any real power or in-tegrity. The good news, of course, is that either type will probably get to star in a yogurt commercial. So we've got options.

The majority of today's pop culture moms are portrayed as

long-suffering martyrs. A typical pop culture mom is pushing forty, attractive *enough* but not overly sexualized (count on her wardrobe to consist almost exclusively of cowl-neck sweaters), and her primary employment is that of a professional buzzkill, endlessly nagging/mocking her infantilized husband. In comedies, the martyr is generally manic and wisecracking (think Julie Bowen in *Modern Family*) or dry and unflappable (see Phylicia Rashad on *The Cosby Show*); just glance to the left of any Judd Apatow leading man and you will find her. In dramas, she is prone to looking tired under harsh lighting (Melissa Leo in *The Fighter*) or belting out harrowing show tunes in close-up (Anne Hathaway in *Les Misérables*). Subspecies of the martyr genus include Saint Mom—a kinder, less ironic version of the standard prototype, whose roots can be traced back to June Cleaver and Donna Reed and who tends to show up in modern times in Meryl Streep romantic comedies (hint: the sight of her pristine eat-in kitchen makes you want to kill yourself)—and Single Mom, who is generally the most bitter of them all, unless she's so desperate to bond with her child(ren) that she attempts to become the elusive Best Friend Mom, typified by that relic of the early aughts, Lorelai Gilmore. Perhaps the most beloved (and committed) martyr of them all, however, is Dead Mom, whose tragic passing paves the way for comedy dads to have hilarious diaper misadventures and for dramatic dads to have sensitive, candlelit sex with models.

And then in the other box we have . . . the MILF. The MILF would make a joke about the fact that I just called her a "box," since "box" is slang for "vagina," and the first rule of being a MILF is that no one can ever forget that you have one, or that you frequently use it for things other than shooting out babies. Whereas the martyr is all about suffering and denial, the MILF lives for celebration and instant gratification. In her purest form— Stifler's mom from *American Pie*, Jane Seymour's pearl-clutching nympho in *Wedding Crashers*, every single Real Housewife on

Bravo—the MILF puts her own needs before those of her kids, generally prioritizing sex above things like eating and sleeping. The purebred MILF is cartoonish and vulgar. She dresses as scantily as possible at all times, preferably in leopard print, and does things like eat bananas in slow motion. She likes to touch her teenage daughter's boyfriends and get drunk at lunch. If the MILF were a man, he would probably end up on *To Catch a Predator*. It *is* possible to be a hybrid of martyr and MILF—see Leslie Mann's career—but to embody both at once is a hollow victory. It tells me—and, worse, the legions of "Girls" out there—that the benchmark of achievement in a woman's postpartum identity is simply to bridge the Madonna-whore gap.

Surely there's more to it than that. I know there is; I'm living it. But I don't think we'll be seeing *Moms* on TV anytime soon, not even on the riskier cable channels. Because somewhere in between the shrews and the vamps there are a million three-dimensional women who just want to take their goddamn bath alone. And who wants to watch that?

OTHER SMALL BUT IMPORTANT ERRORS IN THE HUMAN EXPERIENCE AS DEPICTED IN MOVIES AND TV

The Surprise Coffee

Two characters rendezvous in a public space in a platonic capacity. One character enters the frame holding two generic cups of take-out coffee and hands one of them to the other character. Sample dialogue:

> **Character 1:** Here, I got you coffee.
> **Character 2:** Thanks!

Hold on. Character 1, where did the coffee come from? Starbucks? Dunkin' Donuts? Le Pain Quotidien? The vending machine by the office men's room? Character 2, would this alleged "friend" know your brand likes and dislikes? And even if Character 1 got lucky picking from among these broader coffee distinctions, there is almost zero chance that he could correctly deduce the most crucial and delicate science of coffee enjoyment: Character 2's milk and sugar preferences. I don't even let my *husband* put the milk in my coffee. Character 1 needs to get his ego in check.

The "Regular Booth"

Sorry, group of attractive friends in an ensemble comedy, but ain't no one saving that diner booth for you night after night so you can trade one-liners about your suspiciously low-paying day job that somehow affords you the disposable income to spend eating out every day of your life. Unless you're an unemployed day-drunk at a nearly empty Irish bar, you don't get dibs on a specific seat, and no *way* the management is reserving an entire *table* for you, especially when each member of your party makes his or her dramatic entrance at a different time. God.

The Curious Case of the Six-Month-Old Newborn

[*Screams of pain*]
Doctor: I can see the head! Just one more push!
[*Banshee wail*]
Doctor: It's a girl!

It's also fifteen pounds. Someone get that woman a morphine drip and a pair of drop-crotch pants, stat!

Hospital of the Damned

If you ever find yourself being treated in a hospital staffed only by ethereally beautiful doctors and nurses who have questionable medical ethics and obvious sexual chemistry with each other, rip out your IV and crawl to the nearest free clinic, because chances are four hundred percent that at some point in the near future, a large aircraft / special needs school bus / cruise ship carrying both explosives *and* zoo animals will crash into the waiting room, killing you but sparing the bi-curious anesthesiologist with a pending international adoption.

Sex

I'm not saying humans don't have sex, I'm just saying it's grossly misrepresented on-screen in almost every conceivable way, e.g.:

- I will make a conservative estimate that, in order to preserve a feeling of comic spontaneity or dramatic emotional stakes, seventy-five percent of television and movie characters fall into bed together without expecting to. You almost *never* see a character chatting with her BFF while getting a bikini wax and saying, "I'm seeing Gunther tonight at the office party, so I figured I'd better get rid of these ingrown hairs just in case we

end up boning under the fluorescent lights in the IT cubicle."
In some cases, after the initial hooking up there's an ellipsis
edited in to hide the sex, so I guess it's *technically* possible that
after Sally kisses Harry, she bolts to the bathroom to shave her
legs with an ancient disposable razor she finds stuck to a bar of
soap under the sink, but I harbor suspicions that in fact all
fictional characters keep their genitalia impeccably groomed at
all times, which is just not believable given the amount of time
they also spend killing German spies, battling sudden mon-
soons, changing clothes during montages, convening at their
regular diner booths, and getting each other surprise coffees.

• Two words: bra sex. Yes, I understand: some actresses don't
want to show their aureoles to millions of strangers. I sympa-
thize. But, honestly, when was the last time that a woman having sex in the privacy of her own home failed to remove her
bra? Even if she *wanted* to keep it on, humans are visual crea-
tures, and chances are good that her partner, in the grip of
animal lust, would have stopped at nothing to free her breasts.
Hide them if you must, director, with a sheet or a well-placed
limb, but don't pretend that Victoria's secret is that she can
only climax with the assistance of underwire.

• More characters should get their pants stuck around their
ankles while attempting to swiftly doff their clothing in order
to reveal their sparkling and immaculately manicured privates
to their unexpected sexual conquests. Also, more accidental
armpit-fart noises when glistening bodies rub against each
other in the heat of passion. Incidentally these two details are
my main complaints about *9½ Weeks*.

You Betta Work

*What RuPaul Failed to Teach Me
About Career Choices*

Ask small children what they want to be when they grow up and you will get a variety of adorable, improbable answers. A fairy princess, maybe, or a dinosaur hunter, or a top-ranked cardiologist at the Mayo Clinic. Ask four-year-old me what I wanted to be when I grew up, and I would have brightly responded with my ultimate dream job: New York City bus driver.

Throughout my childhood I *loved* the bus, which is understandable. Buses are very kid-friendly: bouncy, loud, full of the kinds of stimulation that can only be appreciated by people whose brains are not yet fully developed. When we ventured to exotic destinations outside our native Manhattan, via the Port Authority Bus Terminal, I liked to watch the landscape pass by, green trees melting into gray cement with a dancing telephone wire vibrating in between, imagining the awesome power of maneuvering such a spectacular behemoth through the world.

Like so many youthful fantasies, however, I have abandoned this career path as an adult, and not just because I can barely drive a car larger than a Mini Cooper without almost hitting something. No, it goes deeper than that. I've not only lost my appreciation for the trademark sounds and smells of buses but have also in fact come to regard bus travel as one of the deeper circles of hell, a notch or two above being given a jalapeño enema while being forced to listen to an Ann Coulter audiobook.*

This just goes to show that it's hard to know what you want to be when you grow up—even when you *are*, technically, a grown-up. I used to make fun of my mother because, according to her, she's held approximately fifty different jobs. Some people tell their life story in one big lump, but she's preferred to let it out slowly over the years, doling out details like crumbs to my sister and me, who are perpetually starved for gossip, even if it's about our own mom. We survived for *years* on the tidbit that she once was employed making magic wands for a hippie artist on the Lower East Side. "Like, with sparkles and everything?" we asked, half mocking, half delighted. She also worked as a dance teacher, as a bookkeeper, at Greenmarket, at a nursery school. Every year or so a new job comes to light, and we kick ourselves for not pressing her harder for details.

Only recently have I come to realize that I take after my mother, at least in terms of career history. In my seventeen legally employable years, I have held as many jobs. I've never made magic wands, but I did once forge David Arquette's signature on a Bulgarian visa application. So that's something. And I feel like I've learned a few important lessons from casting such a wide net (and making

---

*Why, for instance, do the movies shown on Greyhound buses appear to have been selected by a panel of blind people who have recently emerged from comas? A true story: I was once on a bus from Washington, DC, to New York, and my friend and I had forgotten to bring reading material. As the bus started moving, the driver announced over the intercom that he would be starting a movie momentarily. My friend made an excited noise, at which the intercom once again buzzed to life. "You say that now," the driver cautioned. My friend and I laughed and looked at each other. *How bad can it be?* we asked ourselves. Was there really a movie out there that could make a three-hour bus trip worse? Actually, yes. Its name is *The Adventures of Pluto Nash*. Another time I was subjected to *Agent Cody Banks 2*.

so many egregious errors) while stumbling fearfully along on my haphazard path to becoming a full-time writer.

(By way of a disclaimer, I'm not wearing what would pass in most circles for pants as I type this advice, so you might want to consider that TMI nugget your official grain of salt. You're welcome.)

Your College Major Was (Possibly) a Waste of Time and Resources

If you went to some sort of technical college or trade school, or spend your days operating on cancer patients or building spaceships, then you can skip this section. But if you whiled away four years at a liberal arts college like I did, then you know that every month when you open your student loan bill, the education you're paying for more or less boils down to "how to hold a bong properly while simultaneously making a microwave quesadilla."

Look, *of course* there are valuable academic experiences to be had, and sometimes instead of a quesadilla you make ramen in the mug that you alternately use for an ashtray, but for the most part a liberal arts education is just code for "eh, do whatever." So choosing a major is just a question of deciding what you feel like studying during the hours that you're not binge-drinking or watching other students perform interpretive dance to classic rock songs.

Unfortunately, I did not know this at the time. I thought that choosing my major meant, at age nineteen, selecting the career path I would have to adhere to for the rest of my natural life. The only other indelible decision I made at nineteen was to tattoo an image of Disney's Tinker Bell* on my right shoulder, so I was already 0–1. Things did not look good.

---

*It's in silhouette, and most people assume it's a camel, which is somehow even worse.

I finally chose film studies because I liked watching movies, and while I ended up loving that major, I erred in believing it meant that after graduation I should work in movies for a living. Which brings me to my next two tips.

Never Work for Someone Who Scares the Living Shit Out of You
~ *and* ~
Think Twice About a Job Situated Inside Your Employer's Home

The first job I took after graduation was as a personal assistant to a film producer. I learned about it through the film studies department job board (*Film studies! My* major!!) and interviewed over the phone with a curt, extremely busy-sounding person I'll call Mallory, both to protect her privacy and in honor of the most underrated member of the Baby-sitters Club. On our call, Mallory sounded like she was stuck in a wind tunnel and asked a lot more about how comfortable I was making restaurant reservations than about my favorite example of mise-en-scène in the Hitchcock oeuvre. Still, I did my best to impress her with my passion for what I anachronistically (and pretentiously) referred to as "pictures" and was thrilled when she cut me off, clicked her tongue, and said, with a barely concealed sigh of ambivalence, "Fine, when can you start?"

Signs of trouble were abundant immediately: Mallory would be in L.A. for two weeks, and so I would begin working for her without actually meeting her. My first task would be to move her files and computers from a sleek rented office space in midtown . . . to her ten-year-old daughter's bedroom. Mallory told me that her producing partner had recently relocated to London, so it wasn't necessary for her to shell out for a space anymore.

"That makes sense," I murmured into the phone. I was incredibly self-conscious working out of Mallory's home, a spacious Upper West Side two-bedroom she shared with her daughter and her unemployed, gym-addicted, really, really, *really* gay-seeming husband. I've always felt uncomfortable being left alone in other people's houses, probably because I know I'm not to be trusted. I won't steal or anything, but I'm the type who will taste your food, use your beauty products, look through your photo albums, and try on your clothes—you know, entry-level creepiness. Like Jennifer Jason Leigh in *Single White Female* before she got the haircut.

I got briefly trained by Mallory's outgoing assistant, a friendly girl who always seemed to be covered in a light veil of sweat. She had the frightened, excited air of someone about to be released from prison, which should have sounded an even louder alarm than the fact that I was sharing office space with at least two dozen Barbies. But having never held a real job before, I made myself color-blind to these red flags and busied myself with getting ready for my jet-setting new boss's arrival on the East Coast.

I welcomed Mallory home into her own apartment wearing an ill-fitting suit jacket, bought on sale at Filene's Basement, and jeans, which was my attempt to look effortlessly modern and professional but which came off more like a band leader letting off steam at a truck stop. The first thing I noticed about my employer was her eyes. They were sparkling but flinty and dark, like a patch of black ice on the highway. This, combined with the air-conditioning setting that Mallory preferred, a level I can only describe as "cryogenic freeze," gave me chills, and not in a good way.

There is a difference between someone being intimidating and truly scary. Most bosses are intimidating, just by virtue of the fact that they have more power than you do; specifically, the power to fire you at will. I have always had a healthy fear of authority figures and tend to regard even the most gentle of bosses as a powder keg that could explode in my face at any moment. But Mallory wasn't just imposing; she was fucking terrifying. She gave me a thin smile and dropped her bags in the entryway.

"So get me up to speed," she said, crossing her arms, her defiant smirk telling me that she was already many miles ahead of me, and she knew it.

In the course of my three months at Mallory's, I screwed up constantly—accidentally scheduling a phone conference with two unrelated people, "replying all" to e-mails I was meant simply to eavesdrop on, failing to get her daughter into an after-school swim class. The more useless I felt, the more Mallory seemed to despise me; and the more she resented my incompetence, the more desperate I became. I started finding excuses to leave early, mining past real-life medical emergencies for fodder, even once killing an already-dead grandfather for the sake of a long weekend. But I never found relief. I lived in a constant state of dread, sure that Mallory could tell when I was lying, shuddering at her clipped voice mails instructing me to call her back *right away*. When you begin to flop sweat at the mere idea of speaking to your employer, it's not a great sign. When she went back to L.A. for a long spell at the end of the summer, I was a mess. I binged on entire bags of pricey snacks and then replaced them in a panic. I slathered on her expensive face creams in an attempt to slow the growth of my stress acne. On one particularly low afternoon, I decided to see if I could fit into any of the ten-year-old's designer shorts, then spent the rest of the day searching for hidden nanny cams.

I was finally dishonorably discharged when I gathered up the courage to tell Mallory that I was having a nervous breakdown. I wasn't, actually, but somehow I thought my quitting would make her less angry if I did it with an attitude of pitiful self-loathing. It backfired—she just seemed even more disgusted by my existence. "You should be a waitress," she told me bluntly. I did not take that advice, and the world is a better place for it.

In retrospect, of course, I realize that I was probably an awful assistant completely deserving of Mallory's disdain. But I still maintain that if your boss gives you chronic terror diarrhea, and if you are forced to have that experience on a toilet made by Playskool, then you might be in the wrong job. Just a tip.

Lacking Confidence? Break into Your Dream Job Through the Back Door!

After a few more film-related jobs that ended in humiliation and faked deaths, I decided to reconsider my vocation. I had always loved writing and had recently started a blog, so I did what any young dreamer would do: I took a job as an office manager at an unpopular magazine.

The way I figured it, if I could spend a few years ingratiating myself to the editorial staff, maybe they would let me write something, get my first published byline, without subjecting me to the kind of scrutiny and rejection that writers who send unsolicited queries put themselves through. It was my version of a long con and, to my surprise, it worked, and a lot faster than I had anticipated, thanks to the appointment of a new editor in chief with questionable judgment.

Lars—let's call him Lars—was a charming, unpredictable bon vivant who was quick to laugh, name-drop, and do things like wear French boating shirts to the office, smoke out the window, and get take-out margaritas with his lunch. He was cartoonishly opposite from both Mallory and from the ascetic geeks I'd worked with on various documentary films in between. I loved him instantly, and he took a liking to me, too, mostly because the magazine's owners had informed him, without my knowledge, that I was to serve not only as the office manager but also as his personal lackey. He was easy, though; my errands mostly involved making expensive lunch dates with people whose names I recognized from the gossip column in the *New York Post* or organizing the photos from his most recent trip to Val Kilmer's ranch. After a month or two of ingratiating myself, I painstakingly composed an e-mail asking meekly if he might ever let me write something, and I attached a piece I had recently published on my blog about how much I hated taking the bus. (Did you just get chills from the circle-of-lifeness? Me, too.) Lars gamely threw a few small write-ups my way, and before I knew it I was a published author. The fact that Lars rewrote ninety-eight percent of my prose, making me sound like a wistful, slightly drunk forty-year-old man, did nothing to temper my excitement.

About eight months after I started at the magazine, Lars—who was prone to making business decisions based on emotional attachments—fired the managing editor and gave the job to me. It was the kind of lucky break that you can get only when working for someone given to fits of whimsy and, sometimes, the use of recreational drugs. But I would never be where I am today, sitting on my unmade bed in a Hall and Oates T-shirt, if not for the opportunity he so trustingly and, perhaps, shortsightedly gave me. So thanks, Lars. Your next Dark 'n' Stormy's on me.

Find Out the Hard Way What You Suck At, and Then Don't Do That Thing

For the next five years, I bounced from masthead to masthead. I racked up lots more bylines and got to tell people I was a *magazine editor* in *New York City*, which sounds unfathomably glamorous. If you're picturing Kate Hudson right now, it's okay; so am I.

But, alas, the magazine world I lived in was not a candy-colored rom-com in which I got to wear expensive tailored suits, Louboutin pumps, and a jaunty fedora as I interviewed heads of state in between expense-account trips to decadent sushi luncheons. I didn't even get one of those old-timey PRESS cards to stick in the brim of my cap. In fact, the closest thing I had to credentials was the SEARCHER armband given to me by our building's fire safety marshal, which meant that in the event of a fire, I would have to resist the urge to run out of the building screaming and instead would have to check all the ladies' room stalls for stragglers. (The fact that immediately before my untimely death I might be able to admonish someone for peeing on the seat was cold comfort.)

Anyway, my point is that *Sex and the City* lied to us all. If you work as a magazine or newspaper columnist, you will not be able to afford a single pair of Manolos, let alone three hundred, because you will be too busy hiding loose change in your husband's tube socks to keep you solvent through your next paycheck. But the one thing you *can* do if you work in print is talk to, and occasionally meet, famous people. It's shockingly easy. You just call their publicists and say you work for such-and-such publication. Crazy people, please ignore this next sentence: *they usually do not even check to make sure that you're not lying.* The best part of the process is that the search engine used to find the contact numbers for celeb publicists and managers is called Who Represents [dot] com. When typed out in a URL, it can also be read as Whore Presents.

Given my lifelong obsession with celebrities (when I was an infant, Wallace Shawn lived on my parents' block, and reportedly once snuggled me, so I caught the bug early), you'd think that this easy access to Hollywood's elite would have been a dream come true. But I quickly learned that I was not cut out for the job of speaking to, or meeting, anyone even remotely famous.

To do it well, you have to have the right personality type, which I have since narrowed down to some combination of the following: unrepentant ass-kisser and/or shameless invader of privacy. While I fall into both categories, I am surprisingly ill equipped for celebrity journalism. I blame my rich fantasy life for this. Experienced reporters—even the ones who make a living asking inane questions of pop starlets—treat the experience as a professional task. I, on the other hand, viewed it as an opportunity for the type of meet cute you would normally find in a movie starring the aforementioned Ms. Hudson. Every time I approached an interview, I allowed myself to imagine that the subject and I would totally spark and immediately become BFFs and/or lovers. I once got to eat breakfast with Kevin Bacon (no, I did not order bacon; *God*, you guys, *be cool*), and the whole time I smugly looked around the café, wondering if anyone was taking a secret cell phone shot to sell to *Us Weekly*: "Kevin Cheats on Kyra with Homely Mystery Date Unable to Eat Breakfast Burrito without Burning Crotch with Molten Cheese!"

Celebrities are usually polite, but the more famous they are, the more reticent they will be. Usually they'll repeat the same sound bites over and over, because you are literally the hundredth person to ask them any given question. If you ask something you think is funny or daring, they'll often look confused or annoyed. Also, the written question is much different from the spoken question. You will find yourself tripping over the words that sounded so eloquent and thoughtful on paper, coming off inadvertently as a foreigner who does not understand English contractions. Also, for some inexplicable reason you will feel the need to read them their own biography by way of introduction: *So, you grew up in the Welsh mountains mating cows before moving to Hollywood at age nine . . .* They nod blankly, waiting for the question, but you did your Wikipedia research too well and still have a good paragraph left to go before there is anything approaching punctuation.

Everyone has a word or phrase that they use far too often. For me, with authority figures (or, really, anyone who scares me), this word is "absolutely." If I am asked if something can be done, I say, with confidence, "absolutely." If I overhear an opinion that I agree with even half-assedly, I offer a hearty "absolutely" as a show of my support. And in interviews, any halfway intelligent thing said by the subject is agreed with in this manner. I might say "absolutely"—

with varying degrees of inflection—twenty-five times in the span of ten minutes.

But your matinee idol is not the only person being subjected to your nervous stammering. If you're conducting a phone interview, ninety-nine percent of the time the publicist will be on the call, too. One fabulous exception to this rule was when I received a call directly from Ludacris. "What's up, Una, it's Ludacris," he said by way of introduction. (And he pronounced it flawlessly. Gauntlet thrown, Garrison!) But most of the time you pick up the phone expecting to talk to, say, Dave Coulier,* then hear the telltale echo of speakerphone, followed by, "Hi, it's Jenny! I'm here with Dave. I'll just be listening in. You guys go ahead." Talking to anyone in this scenario would be awkward, but when you are trying desperately to get to know your future paramour and/or best friend who's talking to you long-distance only because he or she is being forced to do so by a third party, it's even worse. Every awkward pause, every failed joke, is magnified by the number of ears listening in. And then, inevitably, "Jenny" cuts in abruptly to "wrap up" your "chat" because "we have other people waiting." Whatever, Jenny. Way to break a girl's heart.

A Nonworking Mother Is an Oxymoron; Anyone Who Says Differently Is Just a Regular Moron

In 2011, I left my job as the managing editor of a weekly New York newspaper in order to birth both a human child and a freelance writing career. One still keeps me up at night, rocking and screaming. And then there's the baby.

Apart from the obvious financial challenges and the fact that I would now have to make or buy my own coffee instead of bogarting the office Keurig machine every two hours, I didn't think too

---

*I have never interviewed Dave Coulier. I wish!

much about what it would mean for my identity to be a woman who works from home and also happens to be a more or less full-time parent. I actually imagined it would be a Django Reinhardt–soundtracked silent film romp in which my son and I took trips to museums, made cookies and got into batter fights, and then collapsed happily for a long siesta, him curled in his crib, and I on the couch with a fresh latte, pounding out masterpieces at five thousand words an hour.

It . . . was not like that.

No one told me how hard it would be. Well, okay, they did. It's just that I, hugely pregnant, well slept and recently showered, throwing back fried mac-and-cheese balls like it was my job (and, by the end, it basically was), didn't hear them. Because I had big plans to HAVE IT ALL.*

I did not feel like I HAD IT ALL as I awoke night after night on the living room floor at four a.m., wearing mismatched socks, one boob hanging out, manually rocking a bouncy seat as I blasted something called "Ocean Waves"—but which I suspect was actually just someone's shitty phone recording of an industrial dryer—while trying to type one-handed on an iPad to meet a deadline. It was rough, and made all the rougher by the fact that people would not stop asking me when I was going back to work.

Let me interject with two disclaimers:

1. Being a parent is full-time work. I know some of you child-less readers are probably rolling your eyes so hard right now—and once upon a time, I was one of you! I was all, *Yeah, sitting at home all day watching* Yo Gabba Gabba! *and playing with toys—cry me a river.* But, dudes. You do not

---

*I feel that this phrase requires all caps because when I think it in my head, it's in the inspirationally angry bark of Coach Eric Taylor from *Friday Night Lights*.

even know. Your day starts when the kid wakes up (note: this generally falls around "ass crack of dawn") and includes zero unsupervised bathroom breaks. Yes, there are fun times to be had, but you will never forget that you are on the clock twenty-four hours a day. You are a one-wo/man nanny, personal chef, chauffeur, maid, court jester, teacher, tour guide, bodyguard, punching bag, and feedlot. It is a *job*. And the salary is zero dollars, ever (actually, the salary is more like negative five million dollars, since you have to pay for your boss's entire existence, for life).

2. Leaving aside whether you want to work outside the home after having kids, it is an insane privilege even to have a choice. Most women in this country, and in the world, don't get to decide whether they want to HAVE IT ALL. So those of us who do are the lucky ones.

That said, I felt judged by the question. When was I going *back* to work? It felt like I was always at work, just not necessarily in locations other people associate with work. Not long after my son was born, I heard through the grapevine that a former coworker of mine—a woman who's incredibly smart and driven and who I looked up to when I worked under her for over a year—was shocked when she heard I wasn't "going back." It made me want to write her an e-mail in HAVING IT ALL caps. I might not have been going back to a cubicle, but I was still valuable, still giving every ounce of my limited reserves of energy and sanity to being a decent human being, good mother, published author, and potential breadwinner. Right?

That was the problem: every defensive pronouncement I made actually ended with a question mark inside my head. I'm still valuable? I'm a productive member of society even if I work in my underpants? Even if I write work e-mails while hovering over a toilet with a screaming baby strapped to my chest? Right? RIGHT,

SOCIETY??? ACCEPT ME!!!!! VALIDATE MEEEEE!!!!! DON'T DEVALUE MY CONTRIBUTION OF ALL THOSE HILARIOUS VAGINA ESSAYS I PUT ON THE INTERNET!!!!!!!!!!

It took me a long time to accept that people will probably never stop asking. That is their right. It is up to me to adjust my own expectations and to admit that while I am a perfectionist with a crippling need to be praised, I also have no desire to work in an office ever again, and I will work my ass off in pursuit of that goal.

I'm a working girl. Like Melanie Griffith, but with fewer cream-colored power suits. I may never HAVE IT ALL, but I hope to have all that I want, which, as of this writing, includes but is not limited to: a successful career; a loving partner (not "husband"—my parents were very sensitive about pronouns, just in case I ever realized I was a lesbian); happy, well-adjusted kids with whom I can spend as much time as I want; the ability to whip up a perfect roast chicken; a top-of-the-line dishwasher that lets me avoid scrubbing any dishes; enviably toned upper thighs; a beach house with a cozy white couch that never gets stained or starts smelling like shellfish; a small dog that rings a tiny bell every time it needs to be walked; hair that doesn't frizz in humidity; preternatural beauty; wisdom; calm under pressure; inner peace; a truly idiot-proof espresso maker; and a good night's sleep.

But until that day, and assuming I never qualify for my bus license, I think I'll stick to writing pantsless on my couch. It's nice work if you can get it.

The 7 Habits of Highly Ineffective People

1. Laziness

I recently Googled my doctor to look up her office hours only to find an article naming her as a *suspect in a Russian prison death*. In the *New York Times*. But then I thought, eh, she already knows the call-in number for my pharmacy, is it really such a big deal?

2. Carbo Loading

Sometimes I try to psych myself up for writing by having a pasta-filled bread bowl, because writing a book is basically like running a marathon, except you don't have to move your legs and you can do it while wearing tooth-whitening trays and slipper socks. But then I get sleepy. And since I'm already in my bed and haven't changed out of last night's pajamas, well, one thing leads to another.

3. Aggressive Retweeting

Those who can, do. Those who are procrastinating from doing, tweet. Those who can't tweet, retweet, and it clogs up my feed and makes me very confused.

4. Overthinking

Okay, e-mail to the boss asking for a raise, let's do this! *Hey, Peter . . .* No, too casual. *Hello, Peter . . .* Oddly formal, almost threatening, like I'm Hannibal Lecter and he's Jodie Foster and he's visiting me in my cell and I'm giving him crazy eyes. *Peter . . . Clarissssse.* Fuck. Now that's all I can think about.

5. Underthinking

P-Dog,

Let's get together and talk about get-
tin' my raise on!

P.S. IT PUTS THE LOTION IN THE BASKET.
LOLOLOLOL

6. Proscrastinatory* Decoupage

Those *Us Weekly* covers aren't going to stick *themselves* to the dining table.

7. Confrontation Avoidance

But we can talk about this later.

*Also: making up words.

I Love You Just the Way You Aren't

In 2008, when we'd been married a year, I made my husband, Jeff, a mix CD. I treated this project as if I were curating an exhibit at the Louvre and finally unveiled it on a long car ride, watching Jeff carefully to gauge what his reaction to each song—and, by extension, the depths of my soul—said about our blessed union.

A summary of my findings:

> **Track 1:** *"I Just Don't Know What to Do with Myself,"*
> *the White Stripes*
> **Sample lyrics:** *I just don't know what to do with myself /*
> *I don't know what to do with myself*
> **Message:** When Jeff and I first hooked up in the spring
> of 2003, the album *Elephant* had just been released, so
> we listened to it pretty much nonstop, mostly while
> getting high and engaging in athletic sexual escapades.
> So it's first and foremost a nostalgia track, attempting
> to encapsulate the helpless feeling of intense lust. But
> we also broke up for six months shortly after getting
> together, so it has a dark underside woven from many
> nights of me crying and eating entire boxes of granola
> bars until I was too gassy to button my jeans.

Jeff's reaction: "Didn't we bone a lot to this?" (Awww. He remembered!)

Track 2: *"Teenage Dirtbag," Wheatus*
Sample lyrics: *I'm just a teenage dirtbag, baby, like you / Ooooh-ooooooooh*
Message: I like obscure bands! There is more to me than Madonna's *Immaculate Collection*!
Jeff's reaction: "You made this mix for *me*, right?"

Track 3: *"Rump Shaker," Wreckx-n-Effect*
Sample lyrics: *I like the way you comb your hair (Uh!) / I like the stylish clothes you wear (Uh!)*
Message: All I wanna do is zoom-a-zoom-zoom-zoom and a boom-boom. (Read: take your clothes off.)
Jeff's reaction: Laughter. (Possibly a reaction to my enthusiastic passenger seat dance moves.)

Track 4: *"Such Great Heights," the Postal Service*
Sample lyrics: *I am thinking it's a sign / That the freckles in our eyes are mirror images*
Message: I lie in bed thinking about your irises and naming our future children.
Jeff's reaction: Skips past song after one second. (I think he may have shuddered.)

(At this point I should mention that almost every song that gives me the warm fuzzies about Jeff turns out to be a song that Jeff hates. "Stay with You" by John Legend comes to mind—back in the summer of 2007 I had what I thought was the great and romantic idea to have a friend sing it at our wedding, so I sat Jeff down and played the song so he could okay it and gave him meaningful looks and held his hand at meaningful times, and at the end he just kind of went, "Eh." In related news, Jeff is a robot.)

Track 5: *"Let's Hear It for the Boy," Deniece Williams*
Sample lyrics: *My baby may not be rich, he's watching every dime / But he loves me, loves me, loves me*
Message: You are not perfect but I love you anyway. You know what else I love? *Footloose.*
Jeff's reaction: Skip (!) "This playlist is for the most effeminate man alive."

Track 6: *"Holding Out for a Hero," Bonnie Tyler*
Sample lyrics: *I need a hero / I'm holding out for a hero till the end of the night*
Message: No, I mean I *really* love *Footloose.*
Jeff's reaction: Skip (!)

Track 7: *"The Tower of Learning," Rufus Wainwright*
Sample lyrics: *I saw it in your eyes, what I'm looking for / I saw it in your eyes, what will make me live*
Message: I think about your eyes maybe more than is normal (see track 4).
Jeff's reaction: Skip. "No."

Track 8: *"It's Always You," Chet Baker*
Sample lyrics: *Whenever it's early twilight I watch 'til a star breaks through / Funny, it's not a star I see, it's always you*
Message: I am sitting outside your bedroom window right now with a boom box, a Peter Gabriel tape, and maybe also some chloroform.
Jeff's reaction: "Awwwww."*

---

*This heartwarming moment was tempered somewhat by the following exchange:
ME: Didn't Chet Baker die young?
JEFF: No, but he was a heroin addict. He hid out in Europe in the sixties and lost all his teeth.

Track 9: *"Cheek to Cheek,"* Fred Astaire
Sample lyrics: *I seem to find the happiness I seek / When we're out together dancing cheek to cheek*
Message: I like either slow dancing with you or doin' da butt. I wish the lyrics were more specific.
Jeff's reaction: Smiles, hand on my knee.

Track 10: *"Let's Get It On,"* cover by Jack Black from High Fidelity *soundtrack*
Sample lyrics: *Let's get it on*
Message: Let's get it on.
Jeff's reaction: "Stop it, I'm trying to drive."

The first birthday gift Jeff ever bought me was a glass head, the kind electronics stores use to showcase headphones. He worked at Pier 1 at the time, and he told me he got me "the weirdest thing" that the store sold. Keep in mind we had only been dating for a few months and he was presenting me with a head-size box. Ah, the red flags ignored by young lovers.

A few years later, when we were living together, I returned the favor by purchasing ten polystyrene mannequin heads for Jeff on eBay. He was going through a phase with his photography wherein he was obsessed with taking pictures of two things: raw meat and mannequin parts (again: red flags). I thought about getting him some steaks, but that seemed unromantic. Luckily, he loved the heads. He stored them in our office closet along with our mullet wigs and Christmas ornaments. Without fail, every December when I went looking for tree lights I would startle upon finding ten white faces staring out at me. It was like living in the movie *Cocoon*.

In those salad days, we let a lot slide. I turned the other cheek when he hung cow eyeballs from a tree for another "project" and forgave him one night when he compared my pubic hair to one of the Little Rascals; in turn, he accepted my idiosyncrasies, such as my habit of getting tipsy and rearranging furniture, my compulsion to hoard and wear his boxer briefs when I ran out of clean underwear, and my tendency to occasionally throw out dishes when I didn't feel like washing them. Over years of dating, we cultivated our intimacy until it was so bizarre and specific that it all but guaranteed no one else would ever want us.

For example, there's a scene in one of our favorite movies, *National Lampoon's European Vacation*, in which Chevy Chase's Clark W. Griswold is counting ballots in an ad hoc election for "president" of the family. "That's *two* for Clark," he says with a smug smile as he reads the last vote. I'm not sure exactly when it started, but at some point around the four-year marriage mark, every time Jeff had more than one bowel movement in the course of a single day, he would emerge from the bathroom with a swagger and proudly announce, "That's two for Clark!" This on top of our *already established* sign language for having just pooped,

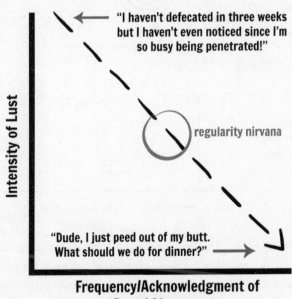

which is to raise both arms in the air like a football ref calling a good field goal. We are truly ruined for all others, so we have no choice but to work on the marriage we have.

Before we had a child, Jeff and I didn't fight very often, and when we did it was over things like which was lamer: engaging in an *America's Next Top Model* Fantasy League or watching *MythBusters* while playing Internet war games. Literally the biggest altercation we'd had in years was over an incident in which Jeff had moved an errant Tootsie Roll from the floor of the kitchen. It wouldn't have been a big deal except that, unbeknownst to Jeff, I had *seen* the Tootsie Roll on my way to the bathroom to brush my teeth and made a mental note to eat it on my way back to bed.

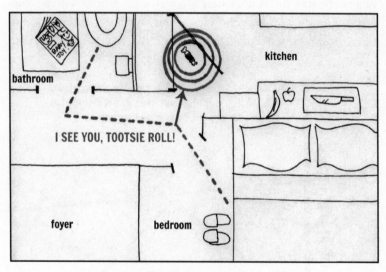

Dramatic reenactment. Or, reendrawment.

I was *so excited* in the bathroom. What could have been rote activities like washing my face, examining my neck for new wrinkles, or poking floss at the inch-wide gaps between my crumbling teeth were elevated to new heights of enthusiasm knowing that I had a chewy little brown morsel awaiting me en route back to the boudoir.

But when I finally returned to claim my prize *it had disappeared*. I began to experience symptoms of what my fifth-grade self might have referred to as "a titty fit."

"What did you do to my Tootsie Roll?!" I wailed to Jeff, who was standing in the bedroom shirtless and displaying unmistakable *boom-chicka-wah-wah* eyes.

"Um, what?" he asked, backing away ever so slightly.

"I saw a Tootsie Roll on my way to the bathroom and I was going to get it on my way back! I made a mental note!!"

The *boom-chicka-wah-wah* faded, replaced by a look of abject terror last seen on the faces of passengers aboard commercial towing spaceship *Nostromo* when a shrimplike alien burst through John Hurt's chest cavity.

"The Tootsie Roll *on the floor*?" he asked.

"Um, *duh*." I am well versed in the art of foreplay.

"I put it back in the *bowl full of Tootsie Rolls* in the pantry." For the record, he said "bowl full of Tootsie Rolls" like they were *all the same*.

"But I was going to pick it up! I *made a mental note*!!!"

"Why didn't you pick it up then?"

"BECAUSE I WAS SAVING IT!!!!"

"For what?"

"AS A REWARD!!!!"

"For . . . peeing?"

"FOR BRUSHING MY TEETH!!!!"

"That . . . makes no sense."

I then gave Jeff my best if-you-want-to-see-boobs-tonight-bring-me-my-goddamn-midgie eyes. And, because he was and is a good husband, he put it back on the tile for me. I now realize that watching your wife pick up and then gnaw on a Tootsie Roll she finds on the floor after a temper tantrum is not generally an aphrodisiac. But I think at this point, Jeff takes what he can get.

So that was then. For years we had the time and energy to spend arguing over who ate or moved whose secret hoard of junk food, or whether we should get stoned, have sex, and then watch the *Planet Earth* episode about seasonal forests, or get stoned, watch the *Planet Earth* episode about seasonal forests, and *then* have sex. Now, we high-five when we both remember to buy toilet paper.

Having a child, for our marriage, was sort of like reversing *The Wizard of Oz* so that instead of stepping off the broken-down porch of the farmhouse and into a candy-colored world of endless possibilities, Dorothy gets bitch-slapped by a Munchkin and thrown back up into the eye of the tornado. I want to stress that it is not like this for everyone, and that we both love each other, and our son, to an extent that is possibly not healthy. But we were a straight, codependent line that was forced to become a triangle, and so we had some . . . growing pains. As such, our fights these days can be roughly divided into five categories.

1. Whose Life Is Worse

Have you ever seen the show *Queen for a Day*? Unless you were born before 1950, the answer is probably no, so let me briefly recap: On this TV show, women would compete to see who had the most hardships, and an *applause-o-meter* would decide which one of them won. These women would break down sobbing while describing their destitution, hunger, crippled children, etc., but only the *saddest* one would win a new dishwasher and get to sit on a throne during the credits. Isn't that so fucked-up?

And yet, Jeff and I have been playing a heated game of Queen for a Day for over two years, except our lists of hardships include things like "chapped nipples" and "can't smoke pot in the house."

2. Who Is More Tired

This is sort of a continuation of Queen for a Day, but with added bouts of dramatic narcolepsy. *Oh, Jeff, I see you've face-planted onto the sofa at seven p.m. still wearing your coat. Hm, interesting. Excuse me while I just fall asleep on the toilet while brushing my teeth with a tube of diaper rash cream. Your move, Rip Van Winkle.*

3. Who Is Less Interested in Sex

At some point, especially when sharing responsibility for a small child, even the most passionate of lovers will begin to find the idea of sex too exhausting to consider. But since no one wants to shoulder the blame for a carnal flameout, I have found that it becomes a game of chicken to see who can disgust and/or avoid the other person more.

"I'm horny," I'll announce, applying acne cream while absentmindedly picking the gnarled bundles of hair off my fleece sweatpants.

"You want a piece of this?" Jeff will yawn, gesturing to his body with his eyes closed. He will invariably be wearing old boxer briefs and a T-shirt he got from the busboy at the Indian restaurant down the street, which is hand-illustrated with a Sharpie.

"Totally, but I forgot to shave." I turn and wink at him, trying to ignore the Pretzel M&M's scattered across his chest. "I hope you like stubble."

"Rrrrowr," he growls. Then, a pause. "I'm *gassy*."

"I bet you are, bad boy. Did you eat Chipotle for lunch again?"

Burp. "I'm gonna go to the bathroom. But then get ready, 'cause you're in trouble." At this point, he can hardly move.

"Why don't we cuddle for a while, set the mood?"

"Mmm-mmmm."

Within seconds, we are asleep on opposite sides of the bed, happily at a stalemate.

4. Whose Turn It Is to Comfort Our Child
in the Middle of the Night

It's hard to summon the neurological clarity to fight while asleep, but Jeff and I do a pretty good job. Something about a child's inconsolable wailing jump-starts the brain's Blame Center, I think.

"The baby's awake," Jeff will groan.

Swimming up from the depths of my slumber, I cannot comprehend this sentence. "No, he's not. He can't be awake. I just put him down."

"Well, he is. . . ."

"Baaaaahhhhhh Fuck. Fuuuuuuck. Fuck everything."

At this point, Jeff usually rolls over and plays dead, and I am forced to resort to bribery.

"Can you go? I'll give you a hundred dollars."

No response.

"Jeff?"

"I think he's hungry."

"No, he's not. You're being an asshole."

After a few of these incidents, we transitioned to a family bed, which conveniently killed two birds with one stone, as having a child sleep between us ensures we can never have sex again.

5. Whose Emotional Response to Stress Is
Correct, aka Who Is More of a Sociopath

Picture Ramona Singer from *The Real Housewives of New York City* after two bottles of wine and a wasp sting interacting with Buster Keaton and you will get a sense of how Jeff and I complement each other emotionally. Sample dialogue:

Me: I am having feelings.
Jeff: . . .

Me: You are not validating my feelings.

Jeff: . . . ?

Me: Now my feelings are that you are a dick. On top of my original feelings.

Jeff: I'm sorry?

Me: What are you sorry for, being a dick or not supporting me emotionally? *

Jeff: . . .

Me: [collapses in sobs]

Jeff: I love you?

Me: Why would you say that to me right now??

Sometimes I feel like we're one of those cutesy news stories at the back of *People* magazine, about how a tiger cub and a tortoise have become best friends at the zoo. The pictures are always adorable, but then you're, like, *This cannot end well. It goes against nature. What will happen when they grow up, and one of them eats the other?* And then, through the gloom, there's that little optimistic Jiminy Cricket voice that chirps, *Y'know, maybe love really does conquer all.*

The jury's still out, though. I might decide to eat Jeff one of these days. He's got this really delicious Chipotle musk going on.

⌒

I was going to end this essay with a new, incredibly meaningful mix tape for Jeff, but when I asked him if he knew any good songs that could be about marriage, he suggested the made-up titles "I Love You, 'Cause You're There" and "Are You Dead Yet?"

So instead, I'll make up a ditty of my own: "I Love You Because."

A few weeks ago, Jeff discovered my supersecret time-saving

---

*This is a trick question, as they are *the same thing*.

method of shuffling to the bedroom from the bathroom with my pants around my ankles.

Allow me to explain:

If I'm about to go to bed and stop in the bathroom to pee, knowing I'm going to take my pants off anyway when I get into my pj's, I don't pull them back up after urinating, choosing instead to scamper the four feet or so into the bedroom in a compromised state. Amazingly, somehow, this dart of shame was like Halley's Comet, and Jeff had never seen this, and when he caught me he burst out laughing.

"Do you love me anyway?" I asked.

Jeff just looked at me and smiled. "I love you *because*," he said.

So, what do you know? Ten years later, romance can still catch us with our pants down.

A Brief Series of One-Act Plays
Between Spouses

Once upon a time in marriage, probably not that far away . . .

Me: Are you okay?

Jeff: [*grunt*]

Me: Is there something on your mind? You look like you have feelings that need to come out.

Jeff: [*silence*]

Me: Do you need to make an emotional fart?

Jeff: [*laughter*]

Me: Just let it rip. Like a heart fart. A ff*heart*!

[*Long pause*]

Jeff: He who felt it, dealt it.

Me: It's weird, when I used to think about having a baby, I never thought about sharing it with someone else.

Jeff: [*immediately*] I get the top half.

Me: No, that's not what I meant. I just never imagined being able to relinquish control to another—

Jeff: Okay, I get the front half.

Me: Stop it, we are not dividing the baby. I'm talking conceptually.

Jeff: Fine, I get the head and extremities. You can have the torso.

Me: I feel like I apologize too much.

Jeff: [*side-eye*]

Me: I'm serious. I'm always saying sorry [Ed. note: often deservedly]. Can we come up with something else I can say, that still means "I'm sorry"?

Jeff: [*after zero seconds of hesitation*] Poop stain.

Me: Oh. Um. Ha-ha. Okay. I was thinking something more inside-jokey and less skidmarky, but okay. What about you?

Jeff: [*side-eye*]

Me: You should have to say something when you're sorry, too. Something you would never normally say.

Jeff: Fine. What?

Me: You have to say . . . Rachel Zoe.

. . . and they never apologized to each other ever again.

How to Be a Perfect Parent in Five Easy Steps, or Never

I don't dole out much parenting advice as a rule, largely because I have only one child, who isn't even old enough to spell, much less shout creative expletives at me, and I still spend most of my days feeling like a complete and utter fraud and failure.

Before Sam was born, I fetishized parenthood as a kind of beatific state that involved a lot of staring down at a swaddled, sleeping child while visitors arrived bearing gifts of wine and foot-long sandwiches.

It doesn't help that my mother has what is either the world's most selective memory or the patience of Job waiting in line at the DMV. She was one of the original attachment parents, a baby boomer brought up in an emotionally barren household who had attended many years of Reichian therapy in pursuit of her goal to love and bond with my sister and me to an absurd degree.

This meant that I was held constantly, that I slept in bed with my parents well into kindergarten, and that I breast-fed until I was four years old. (Or five, maybe. My mom has always been fuzzy on the exact math, but I choose to go with four, because as it is, people tend to look so shocked that I'm afraid their lower jaws might actually fracture were I to add a full year to my tenure of latching on to what I liked to call "nippy.") Mom says she tried to convince me to wean at age two, but that I refused, arguing, "But, Mommy, I like it." Incidentally, this is also why I refuse, as an adult, to go on any diet that excludes alcohol.

When I ask my mother if any of her sacrifices—being regularly kicked in the face during slumber, being suckled like a Holstein into her forties—took a toll, she always smiles brightly and tells me that she loved every minute. So that's how I entered into motherhood. Completely excited, naively confident, and totally fucking deluded.

To say that my first weeks as a mother failed to live up to my expectations would be a staggering understatement. First of all, in my visions of postbaby rapture, I always pictured myself in a flattering maxidress that clung to my newly bountiful cleavage in a manner that would remind my guests of Halle Berry emerging from a waterfall in a string bikini. Instead, I wore what amounted to a diaper made of enormous maxipads, held up with mesh boxer briefs.

I also, freakishly, lost my appetite, so the plentiful gifts of banana breads, casseroles, and lasagnas were wasted on me. I didn't glow; I withered. I looked pale and sad. I was too tired to do much besides sit on the couch holding my son and looking overwhelmed. My skin broke out and my nipples, which had up to that point never had to work a day in their lives, literally cracked under the pressure. Approximately eight thousand times a day, after feeding my mewling little miracle, I would alight to the kitchen, where I would carefully dip my breasts first in salted water and then in olive oil. It was sort of like making a sexy bruschetta (aside from the scabs) and it was the closest I came to cooking for a good twelve weeks.

There *were* bright spots: I rewatched all of *30 Rock* and *Mad Men* and *Lost* over the course of a month, while sitting and breastfeeding like a really lazy martyr, Our Lady of Perpetual Hulu. I eventually stopped needing adult diapers and didn't have to wear a bra most of the time. I automatically got free two-day shipping with Amazon Prime just for expelling another human being from my body. It wasn't all bad. And of course, I loved my newborn son so much it consumed me. It was like a tidal wave of hormones I drowned in, for better or worse. It's true that for about six weeks I cried whenever the sun set and that I did once add Brooke Shields's *Down Came the Rain* to my Amazon cart for overnight shipping. But I didn't end up ordering it. Postpartum depression is a serious illness, one that I thankfully did not have. What I had, I came to understand over time, was the normal reaction to becoming a new parent, which can be boiled down to a single, haunting refrain: *What in the fuck have I done?*

No matter how much you love your baby (and all the clichés are true—it's like your Grinch heart grows five hundred sizes and then you put on permanent, person-specific beer goggles for the rest of your natural life), there is no way to prepare for the nanosecond during which you transform from a freewheeling childless narcissist into someone who is responsible for protecting, nurturing, and educating a helpless, wailing flesh peanut for the next eighteen years and then, oh yeah, also, *forever*.

Time-out: If you're tripping over the words "freewheeling" or "narcissist," thinking something along the lines of, *Hey, that's not me. I worked eighty-hour weeks! I built igloos out of recycled small-batch soda bottles for Habitat for Humanity! I'm a self-hating vegan monk with agoraphobia! How dare you judge me?! You're just a virgin who can't drive!!* Okay, first of all? I took care of those last two bucket list items at ages twenty and twenty-five, respectively, so how do you like them freakishly old apples? Second, no matter how hardworking or self-denying or altruistic you think you were before you had kids, I guarantee you that your life was actually one hundred thousand times more indulgent than you think. For example, did you set your own alarm clock, and did it ever hit you? Did you consider it a basic human right to be able to poop alone, without being stared at? Did you ever give more than a fleeting moment's thought to anyone else's naps? Did you do things like drink a cup of coffee or read the news without having to turn on the TV at top volume to distract someone who otherwise would be literally trying to eat your body? The defense rests. Which, of course, is just a figure of speech, since I haven't had a good night's sleep in years.

But back to the moment of birth. It's life altering in an almost comically overdramatic way, like the Kool-Aid man crashing through the wall of your otherwise humdrum barbecue.* You give up your former life cold turkey, and then sweat through the withdrawal for a few months (or, in my case, years). I hope this doesn't make it sound like I hate being a mother—I don't, at all, and I wouldn't go back to a life without my son even if I could (as it is, my birth canal resembles one of those air mattresses that will never, ever be able to fit entirely back into its pouch, no matter how aggressively you deflate it). But loving a child and even fetishizing parenthood won't protect you from a bone-chilling, existential angst that can set in within seconds of delivering the placenta.

This is the voice that will keep you up nights, asking questions like, *Who approved you to be a parent? I have seen you lick pudding off your cell phone, and you weren't even sure it was pudding at the time!* Or, *Is the baby breathing? No, but really, is he? If you look really close? Is he pooping enough? Is he pooping too much? Is his poop the right color? Is my breast milk less healthy because I ate twenty-five Mary Janes for lunch yesterday? Does it taste like the milk at the end of a bowl of Lucky Charms? Is he sleeping enough? Is he sleeping in the*

---

*This is also what vaginal childbirth feels like, from a structural standpoint.

right position? If I pick him up every time he cries, will he be too de-pendent? If I don't pick him up, will he be a sociopath? Is there any way I can find out what Tom Hanks's mother did, and then also Jef-frey Dahmer's, so that I can make an informed decision about sleep training? Speaking of which, is it weird that he's always trying to bite my face? If he turns out to be a cannibal, will I still love him just as much as if he were a urologist or a model?

There aren't any answers—not immediately, anyway. Other new parents are just as freaked out and useless, and people with older kids have repressed the first few months; they'll probably just hand you a lasagna and then find an excuse to leave the room. Also, forget the Internet. I'm serious. Until you regain the ability to reason that comes with at least five hours of consecutive sleep, online message boards are not your friend. If you doubt me, stop reading right now and type any infant-related worry into Google. Now tell me how long it takes before some stranger is informing you that you need to go to the ER, usually in frantic, misspelled ALL CAPS, because, presumably, the sanatorium only gives them computer privileges for five minutes at a time.

So, while I've never liked the phrase "fake it till you make it," as depressing as it is, that's really what child rearing boils down to: pretending you know what you're doing while secretly suspect-ing that you—you *specifically*—are the person Keanu Reeves was talking about in *Parenthood* when he says, "You need a license to buy a dog, or drive a car—hell, you need a license to catch a fish. But they'll let any butt-reaming asshole be a father." Only, substi-tute "mother" for "father" if you're a woman. You get it.

⌒

Of course, not everyone is willing to admit that they don't know anything. Why would they, when there's money to be made by exploiting our rampant insecurities? There are loads of people out there writing books and articles and studies and blog posts about how to get your baby to sleep through the night at eight weeks, use a potty as something other than a hat, or signal for more macaroni in Morse code, and all of them make it seem easy, and like *you're* the asshole for not pulling up your sweatpants and wiping away your pudding stains (it was definitely pudding . . . I'm at least ninety percent sure) and just doing it already. *This is the secret to fixing your entire life,* these self-anointed experts coo.

At first I believed them. I bought their books. I bookmarked their articles. Occasionally I even read a sentence or two in between nipple dips and Hulu ads. I tried things like nursing on all fours to avoid plugged milk ducts, wrapping the kid like a burrito and then holding him like a football. I even bought blackout curtains for our bedroom that made it look like Meat Loaf's castle in the "I'd Do Anything for Love" video. None of it did any good. Looking back from a relatively sane perspective, I think there are two reasons for this:

1. At the time, I defined successful results as "magically transforming my life back to normal." Little did I know, the ship of normalcy had sailed the moment a human head emerged from my lady bits. And you know what? In retrospect, that was a pretty big red flag.

2. The people who wrote the books and articles and blog posts meant well, but the advice they were doling out was usually specific to one type of child—*theirs*. When you're a parent and you accidentally discover something that works, you basically do handsprings and then go outside to leap at strangers in the street for Milli Vanilli–style chest bumps. You become filled with the misguided confidence that everyone can benefit from your experience, and then you write a book about it. (Not that *I* would ever do that. Ahem. Let's move on.)

Since none of the tried-and-true baby-whispering tricks worked for me, I was left to my own devices, and by "devices," I obviously mean the various remote controls to my TV and Roku box. This is why, for a few weeks in early 2012, I thought I had discovered the secret to baby sleep. And that secret's name was Ryan Gosling.

Here's how it happened: One night in February, for no apparent reason, my previously catnapping baby was unconscious for eight hours straight. This was a Very Big Deal in my household, and the subject of much jubilation—that is, once I confirmed that he was, in fact, still alive when I awoke with a terrified start and two Heidi Montag–size breasts at seven a.m.

I practically skipped around the following day, throwing my hat up into the air à la Mary Tyler Moore, telling anyone I could find that my life was about to change.

I was an idiot. That night we maxed out at three consecutive hours. The next night, four. I wracked my brain for any conceivable reason for our one-off success. I kept trying to re-create the circumstances of the night I'd started referring to as "Armabeddon," going so far as to eat the exact same dinner of salami and cheese on a few slices of stale bread, washed down with the same two glasses of the same cheap red wine. I even dressed the baby in the same pajamas he'd been wearing that night, on the off chance that they were made not by popular child's clothing brand Zutano but rather by magical elves who lived on a diet of Benadryl and soft ocean waves.

No such luck. "You fools!" my infant seemed to sneer, like Vizzini in *The Princess Bride*. "You fell victim to one of the classic blunders: never go in against a four-month-old when *sleep* is on the line!"

And then, just when my husband and I were about to throw our hands up and call it a freakish anomaly, *he did it again*.

Now we had two sets of data to compare, and, after painstakingly retracing our steps, we discovered something wonderful: the only thing the two nights had in common was that we had watched movies; specifically, *The Ides of March* and *Drive*, which both star Ryan Gosling.

Then it was game fucking *on*. That night I happily paid to download *Blue Valentine* in HD, mentally designing the cover of my bestselling book *The Gosling Solution: Hey, Girl, Get Your Baby to Sleep Through the Night Using the Magical Powers of the Guy from* The Notebook. Jeff and I opened another bottle of wine, toasted to our genius, and proceeded to watch a supremely depressing two-hour movie about how all people are broken and all marriages are doomed. Ten minutes later, Sam woke up.

How dare you, Ryan? I was going to be bigger than Ferber.

⌒

If you've learned one thing from this chapter so far, it is probably that I'm not really qualified to give parenting advice (information, you may remember, that could have been gleaned from the very first sentence! I wanted to give you an excuse to phone it in during book club so you could focus on the cheese plate). That said, I do have some nonpatronizing* tips for ignoring / putting in perspective all the *bad* advice that's out there.

You Will Always, *Always* Be Doing Something Wrong . . . So Stop Worrying About It

In case you *don't* know what you're doing wrong, I have provided a handy chart.

---

*Unless you have more than one child, in which case you know all this already and are probably giving me the "talk to the hand" gesture, because in my mind it is forever 1994.

A Brief Index of Common Parenting Mistakes and Their Meanings

Are you . . . ?	Then, obviously . . .
Exclusively breast-feeding	THE BABY WILL NEVER SLEEP THROUGH THE NIGHT AND YOUR NIPPLES WILL FALL OFF, AND YOU'LL HAVE NO ONE TO BLAME BUT YOURSELF.
Exclusively formula-feeding	YOU'RE POISONING YOUR BABY, YOU MONSTER. DO YOU EVEN KNOW WHAT'S IN FORMULA? PRETTY MUCH JUST FECAL MATTER AND SCRAP METAL.
Sleep training	YOU'RE ABANDONING YOUR BABY AND AS A RESULT IT WILL NEVER FORM A PROPER EMOTIONAL ATTACHMENT TO ANOTHER HUMAN BEING.
Not sleep training	YOU'RE CODDLING YOUR BABY AND AS A RESULT IT WILL DEPEND ON YOU FOR THE REST OF ITS NATURAL LIFE.
Cosleeping	IF YOU DON'T ACCIDENTALLY KILL YOUR BABY BY SMUSHING IT IN THE NIGHT IT WILL PROBABLY GROW UP TO BE A SEXUAL DEVIANT.
Introducing solids at four months	YOU MUST WANT YOUR BABY TO CHOKE TO DEATH, DON'T YOU?
Still feeding your one-year-old purees	YOU MUST BE A COMPLETE AND TOTAL PUSSY.
Making your own baby food	WHAT, MORTAL FOOD ISN'T GOOD ENOUGH FOR YOUR PRECIOUS BABY, GWYNETH?
Not making your own baby food	CONGRATULATIONS, YOUR CHILD HAS JUST INGESTED ITS OWN WEIGHT IN ARSENIC.

Are you . . . ?	Then, obviously . . .
Using disposable diapers	YOU MUST WANT TO SPEED UP GLOBAL WARMING WITH THOSE LITTLE SHITBALLS OF ETERNAL WASTE.
Using cloth diapers	OH, HELLO, HIPPIER-THAN-THOU MARTYR WHO DOESN'T OWN A TV!
Using plastic of any kind, ever	SEE: NOT MAKING YOUR OWN BABY FOOD
Letting your kid play in dirt / eat sand / lick playground equipment	WAY TO PLAY TRICHINOSIS ROULETTE, PIGPEN.
Purelling the (literal) living shit out of your child	YOU'RE KILLING ALL THE GOOD BACTERIA AND DAMNING YOUR KID TO A LIFE OF NOT BEING ABLE TO DIGEST ANYTHING BUT SPELT BREAD.
Going back to work and hiring a nanny	YOUR CHILD WILL PROBABLY GROW UP CALLING YOU BY YOUR FIRST NAME.
Staying home with your kid	YOU'RE NOT CONTRIBUTING ANYTHING TO SOCIETY. LEAN IN, GOD DAMN IT. LEAN INNNNN!!!
Engaging your baby in educational play every waking moment	YOU'RE A HOVERING PSYCHO WHO'S SABOTAGING ANY HOPE OF YOUR CHILD LEARNING TO BE INDEPENDENT.
Letting your child watch *MythBusters* while you blog and drink a half bottle of wine	YOU'RE A NEGLIGENT SLOTH WHO'S SABOTAGING ANY HOPE OF YOUR KID GETTING INTO A DECENT COLLEGE.
Sending your kid to private school	YOUR CHILD WILL GROW UP IN A PRIVILEGED BUBBLE AND BECOME THE KIND OF OUT-OF-TOUCH ASSHOLE WHO WEARS A BOW TIE TO FOOTBALL GAMES.

Are you . . . ?	Then, obviously . . .
Homeschooling	YOUR CHILD WILL BECOME THE KIND OF ANTISOCIAL WEIRDO WHO BUILDS HIS OWN YURT AND MAILS ANTHRAX TO POLITICIANS.
Sending your child to public school	YOUR KID WILL BARELY LEARN HOW TO SPELL SINCE SHE'LL BE TOO BUSY MAKING SHIVS OUT OF ASBESTOS SHARDS.

So ask yourself, what has four thumbs and is fucking up his or her offspring no matter what? You and me, baby! Now give me a high five and let's go do some more unwitting damage to those precious little angels.

To Sleep, Perchance to—Nope. No Chance. Give Up Now.

(See also: the betrayal of Ryan Gosling, recounted earlier.)

Sleeping through the night doesn't seem like such a hard task. Not to brag, but I used to do it all the time. One minute I would be struggling to decode a Will Shortz pun, the next minute: Sunlight! Garbage trucks! Some jerk honking! A new day dawned.

Babies, however, appear not to have gotten the memo. There is no kind way to say this: they sleep like assholes.

There is literally nothing you will obsess about more in the first year of parenthood than your child's sleep patterns. At social gatherings, it will be all you can talk about. You'll want to know who's getting it, how often, and how deep. *How long does it last?* you'll ask friends breathlessly over cocktails. *Twenty minutes? Three hours? Six?* Sleep is to the rest of your life what sex was to your twenties: you talk about it much more often than you do it, and your roommates present a considerable obstacle.

At home, more tired than you ever thought possible, you will read studies in small print by the light of your iPhone. You will make logs of night wakings only to find in the morning that you accidentally used a lo-mein-encrusted chopstick and a DVD case to record this vital information. You will volunteer nap schedules—without prompting—to total strangers. You will study the creaky floorboards in your house like a military operative searching for land mines in Afghanistan.

I can't stop you from doing this. However, I *can* tell you that no matter how your child sleeps or how you choose to address it, sleep for everyone will probably suck for the first year at least. If you don't sleep train (i.e., suffer through the dreaded "cry-it-out"), it will suck because it's unpredictable and erratic, and if, like me, you give up and let the kid into your bed, you run the risk of getting head-butted in the night. If you *do* sleep train, it will suck because you'll be sentenced to live out the same schedule over and over, like Bill Murray in *Groundhog Day* only with less imminent death (and sleep-trained babies love to relapse, especially during tropical vacations). So chill. It sucks for everyone. Find peace in the knowledge that you can't really fuck up baby sleep, because it is *inherently* fucked. Anyone who says otherwise is not to be trusted.

Your Life Will Resemble a Michael Myers Movie More than a Nancy Meyers Movie

Thanks to a brain steeped in decades of neat and tidy pop culture parenting, I believed for the first few months that it was only a matter of time before I was back to my old self—having weekly drinks with girlfriends, wearing clothes not exclusively made of jersey, sipping lattes and buying baguettes while somehow pulling off a beret and then returning home to type away on my laptop for hours. Never mind that my life had never been like that to begin with. I stuck my fingers in my ears and indulged in hallucinations of motherhood as a shiny, happy montage of HAVING IT ALL-ness, with a child who would fit right in as the adorable, character-building sidekick who would dance with me in the kitchen to upbeat Motown songs while we made cupcakes and licked the batter off the spoons. Everyone needs life goals, and mine, apparently, was a Kate Hudson movie.

I don't even think I included "showered every day" or "didn't cry once for a whole half hour" in my fantasy, because those were givens in my rosy, perfect life, in which the fridge would overflow with bowls of ripe organic fruits, and someone else's poop would *never* accidentally get on my pants.

[Needle-screech-on-record sound effect.] Ha-ha, no. Parenthood is basically the opposite of everything I just said. Of course there are plenty of transformative moments, but those generally take place when you are on the toilet by yourself. The rest of it is messy, both physically and emotionally. You will survive it, but it will not always be pretty. *This is normal.*

It Pays to Treat Your Partner Like Doug E. Doug

My relationship with my husband, Jeff, was rock solid before our son came along. We used to be able to say things to each other like, "Okay, today's agenda is: smoke pot, have sex, and get haircuts. Which order should we do them in?" We loved spending time together but we also relished our time apart. We thought we would make the coolest parents.

Then the baby came, and our marriage, like everything else, changed completely overnight. I'm not going to lie, during the first few years we took a few detours into some Edward Albee territory. Sneers and eye rolls replaced high fives and steamy make-out sessions. Suddenly, all the attention and patience and affection we used to save for each other was going to the baby, and things often got heated (in the unsexy way). Not everyone will have marriage problems after having kids; don't get scared. But if you do, know that you're going to have to work hard to learn how to nurture the relationship again. Like everything else about parenthood, it will be messy and tiring, but ultimately rewarding and even kind of life affirming. I think it helps when things are bad to think of the two of you as Derice and Sanka from *Cool Runnings*. You're out of your element and up against almost insurmountable odds, but if you maintain a sense of humor and trust in John Candy, you'll make it to the finish line one way or another.

"If Mama Ain't Happy, Ain't Nobody Happy" Sounds Like a Crappy Tyler Perry Movie but Is Also Totally True

All the organic, fair-trade, pasture-raised Play-Doh and eight-hundred-count recycled hemp crib sheets in the world won't matter if you don't feel at least reasonably happy and cared for. This means taking time—by force or even, God forbid, *Yo Gabba Gabba!* if necessary!—to eat, sleep, and do things that matter to you, whether that's work or crappy reality TV or a manicure or a spin class. If you find yourself flailing, or fantasizing about getting into a nonfatal car accident so that you can finally "relax" in the hospital, please get help. See a therapist; get meds if necessary. Or just shell out for a sitter and schedule a night with friends when you can bitch about your problems and get tipsy and feel like the old you again. Whatever gets you to a better place. Your happiness matters. It matters just as much as your child's happiness, because your child's happiness depends on you. Everything depends on you. *No pressure or anything, Jesus.*

But seriously, if there's one thing I want you to take away from this, it's that in two-plus years I have learned really only five things. And one of them is *not* how to stop sleeping in my jeans so often.

On the plus side, I wake up fully dressed. Being a mom is all about shortcuts.

"Daddy!" Zoe squealed.

Rachel peered outside and slammed her fist on the table, rattling the china. "Wait a minute. Is that someone in the car with him? It is! It's a woman." She threw down her napkin and shot up from her chair.

I opened the curtain and saw Anh slinking in the front seat and Michael trying to convince her to get out. This wouldn't end well.

"We'll make room," Noble said cheerfully. "The more the merrier, right, dear?"

"We'll do no such thing," Rachel said, following her daughter out the door.

Anh was resting against the passenger door and Vi was still in her carseat in the back when I reached them.

Zoe rushed to hug her father, and Rachel stopped in her tracks on the sidewalk. "*You!*"

Anh glanced up sheepishly and fingered a wave to Rachel. Michael beamed, oblivious to his ex-wife's reaction. "Great. Everybody's here. But I guess introductions aren't necessary."

Rachel spun on her heel and glared at me. "You knew all along, didn't you? Your best friend was sleeping with my husband and you didn't have the decency to tell me about it. What kind of sister are you?"

Michael took Anh's hand and stared at his ex-wife. "Would it kill you to be happy for me?"

Rachel stuck her nose into the air. "Be nice! Ha! You'll be sorry you ever crossed me! And don't even think about asking me back! I wouldn't take you back if you were the last human on earth!"

Michael smirked. "I don't think that will be a problem. Come on, let's not ruin a perfectly good holiday."

"*Good?* What do *I* have to be thankful for? A jackass husband and a lying, conniving sister who keeps secrets behind my back? Yes, Happy Thanksgiving, indeed! While you're busy ruining my life, is there anything else I should know about?" Rachel stared at me, then Cortland, and back again.

Cortland began to raise his hand, when I slapped it down. "No, I think that will do it for today."

Rachel stomped back into the house. Anh got Vi out of the car seat while Michael began walking up the steps with his daughter. I stayed back and waited for Anh. "For some reason, I thought she'd take the news better."

Anh walked in stride beside me. "Kill me now," she muttered.

Cortland grabbed my fingers, pulling me back so we were the last in line to reach the front porch. "So Rachel broke up with me last night, just before I got the chance."

"So I heard."

"So have you told her you'd like to start seeing me?"

"I don't know if I'd like to start seeing you. Are all doctors this presumptuous, or is it just you?"

He put his hand on my waist, and his forearm next to my head, pushing me back against the brick of the house. "Well, I think you should know our duck house passed inspection. With flying feathers, you might say. I close tomorrow."

"Tomorrow? That's awfully soon, isn't it?"

"When you know what you want, why wait?"

"I suppose I could bake you some cookies as a housewarming gift. To welcome you to the neighborhood and all."

"Cookies? I had something else in mind."

"My father always said patience was a virtue."

"British origin, right? The capacity to accept or tolerate delay, trouble or suffering without getting angry or upset. Yeah, I pretty much suck at that."

"What are you, some kind of walking dictionary?"

"No, but I'm pretty good at defining what I want. Getting it is the tough part."

Our eyes lingered, and I touched his cheek as he leaned in c "We better get inside," I said, my hand pressed against his che:

Cortland stepped back. "I'm going to take off. I've got Linds the weekend. She's going to help me move in."

"Okay, then. I'll see you around."

Cortland began walking down the sidewalk, when he turne "You know when you said that I put people to sleep for a living

"I recall something of the sort."

"Well, just remember that I wake them up, too."

Chapter 23

"Life without love is like a tree without blossoms or fruit."
—*Kahlil Gibran*

ACCORDING TO PSYCHOLOGISTS, 95 percent of people think about sex at least once a day. I belonged squarely within the freakish 5 percent that didn't. Until da Vinci. After that, I thought about sex a dozen times a day—nothing compared to a man, but often for a woman. As I finished up my dissertation to hand in to my professor, I realized I hadn't been missing the physical act of sex. Sure, I'd been missing pleasure, but what I'd missed most was the golden triangle of sex, love and communication. I missed a *real-thing* relationship. I thought After, I'd never be real with anyone again, settling within the uncomfortable typecast of a melancholy widow. It was only after I stepped back into the world of the living again that I could consider loving again.

Author Josh McDowell claims that "I love you" can be interpreted several different ways. One meaning is "I love you *if*," based on what the other person *does*. My sister could love Cortland *if* he lived in a mansion with a heated pool. Another meaning is "I love you *because*," based on what the other person *is:* attractive, strong, intelligent. Da Vinci believed he loved me *because* I was kind to him in a strange new world. *Because* I took him in. *Because* I made him feel safe and warm and wanted.

I wondered if Joel loved Monica solely *because* she was beautiful, but a part of me believed Joel had loved Monica the third way—the same way he'd loved me: unconditionally. She was the one who had betrayed him, had loved him because he was the safe choice, the opposite of her equal partner Jonathon. Perhaps Joel loved her despite her being beautiful. For so long I had wanted Joel to love me more, better, longer, deeper, but after all that's happened, I knew how one could love differently and have it mean as much as the other.

The best and hardest love to achieve is unconditional. *I love you, period.* I love you when you gain twenty pounds, make a mess around the house, and grow black hairs from your moles. I don't just love you until someone better comes along. I love you *forever.*

I knew I had this kind of love with Joel. He didn't just love me until Monica was ready to return to him. He never would've jeopardized what we had. I was ashamed I had thought that he would leave me so easily.

I wanted to release Monica of her guilt before Christmas. Whatever she had to get off of her chest, I was ready and willing to listen. It was the second week of December, the first snowfall salting the earth as I drove to her office to meet her. She was busy as usual, squeezing me in between two appointments. My dissertation was tucked neatly in my portfolio, ready to hand over to the professor after I met with Monica.

I entered the building, visualizing the lines Joel had sketched in creating his work of art. Most architects use computers now, but Joel had been old school. He loved nothing more than his drafting table and a freshly sharpened pencil. I could feel Joel's presence with me as I made my way through the marble corridor to the stainless steel elevator. Monica Blevins, top floor. Of course. Corner office. Nothing but the best.

Her assistant showed me into her office where she was bent over paperwork, black framed glasses on her pretty face, lips as red as beets. She smiled upon seeing me and rose to greet me. "Thanks so much for coming," she said warmly. "I'm sorry we have to meet in a stuffy law office." I admired the exquisite décor and breathtaking view from her floor-to-ceiling window—nothing stuffy about it. I wondered if Joel had known which office would be Monica's, if he had spec'ed in special accommodations for her. It seemed like the sort of thing he would do.

Monica came around the large ebony desk to sit next to me in a matching leather chair. She crossed her legs, long runner's legs with calves that probably sent most men into salivation. She wore four-inch heels, something I'd never even attempted. She kept her gaze on me, and then I noticed her eyes watered. "How have you been?"

I folded my hands into my lap, no longer ashamed that she made me look like a fashion imbecile. I was being me, pressed khakis, a taupe cardigan and one new addition of red patent leather loafers, which remarkably gave me some pep in my step.

"Love the shoes," Monica said, admiring them. "I wouldn't have taken you for a red shoe girl."

"Me, neither," I said. "I've discovered it about myself. I've always been afraid to wear red, so the shoes … well, it's a start."

"A wise choice." Monica said, probably considering whether or not to chitchat. There was so much we could talk about this time of year—holiday plans, what the kids want for Christmas—but I was glad she got right to the point. I'd expect no less of a good lawyer.

"Jonathon told me he saw you," she said evenly.

"He did? Well, I'm glad for that. I wouldn't want to lie."

"Of course you wouldn't. I'm the only liar here. I lied to myself for years. Don't assume that comes with the occupation. I lied to myself about Joel. I thought he would make me a better woman because of who he was. Give me a better life if I stuck with him."

If. Because. I resisted the smile pressing at the corners of my mouth.

"I thought Jonathon could be no more than a fling. But you know what? He loved me even though I repeatedly told him I loved Joel and was going to marry him. He said, 'I don't care what you tell me. I'll never stop loving you. You could lose your looks and get fat and be a five-foot housewife who runs around in a robe all day and I'd still love you.'"

"Not that you would ever do that."

"He knows me too well. But he *said* it, you know? And I just wanted you to know that I'm sorry if whatever I did in Joel's past messed things up between you two. I would understand if he had trust issues or kept himself from truly letting go and loving again."

I shook my head. "You know what? It wasn't that way at all. I don't think he held back. It was me that always wondered. I was jealous. I mean, look at you. But I was wrong to think you were a problem."

"I'm glad you're saying that, because I did try to get in the way of you two. When Joel was designing this building."

My throat tightened, and I held onto my knees to brace myself for the news. "Just say it."

She held my gaze, never wavering. "I kissed him."

I exhaled. "And?"

"And that's all. I kissed him one night after a dinner meeting to see if there was anything left between us."

Imagining the two of them in a soul kiss, made me stomach turn. "And?"

"Nothing. Joel told me he loved you and you were the one he was always meant to be with."

I could feel a tear trail down my cheek. "He said that?"

"He said he never knew how good a life could be. All because of you and the boys."

I nodded, my lips pressed together to keep from going into the ugly cry.

"I'm sorry I kissed him," Monica said.

"I'm not. Maybe your kissing him made him realize the words he was telling you. Maybe you did the right thing by doing the wrong thing."

Monica squeezed my hand. "I never thought of it that way. One last thing before you go. I wanted to give you some kind of proof about Joel—occupational hazard, perhaps—and I remembered I had kept a card he sent me."

I took the opened envelope from her, afraid to put it in my purse, for fear it would disappear. "I never thought I'd be saying this, but thank you, Monica. For everything."

I left her office, my free hand fingering the walls as I did, like a child who couldn't keep her hands to herself, as if touching them were somehow touching Joel. I ran my hands along the hallway, the doors, as the partners looked at me strangely, I turned in circles in the elevator as I touched it, too, while the elderly gentlemen in the three-piece suit grinned. "You must be in love," he said to me as the doors swished open. I put my hand to my heart. "Very much so."

I waited until I was seated in the car to open the envelope. My heart raced at the sight of Joel's neat penmanship.

> *Dearest Monica,*
>
> *I write this because I felt you deserved more than an e-mail or a cold voice mail message. Our past was what it was, but I would not change it. That feels odd to say, but I am in such a good place in my life, and you are obviously happy with Jonathon. I realize now that looking back, you two were always more comfortable together than you and I ever were. Now that I am with the love of my life, I know what it all means. Because Ramona means everything to me, I must respectfully remove myself from the project, but know that you are in good hands with my partners and personally, you are in very good hands with Jonathon. Everything works out for the best.*
>
> *Love, Joel*

I held the open card to my chest, his words pressing against my heart. "I love you, too, Joel. I'll always love you." And instead of looking up into the sky, I looked beside me, where I imagined him sitting in the passenger seat, fiddling with my stereo buttons. He winked at me, and I continued to speak to him. "I'm sorry I ever doubted you. And I promise to be open to feeling you in my life, guiding us, loving us, watching over us."

"You should've known you couldn't get rid of me that easily," he said, and he was gone.

***

I found Dr. Roberts on the stage, gathering up his notes as the swarm of students exited the auditorium. He was a legend—"Word Doc," they called him—with a radio show on NPR and a blog read by thousands each day. Not bad for a man in his seventies.

Clutching my dissertation, I made my way down the aisle until I was looking up at him, my neck craned back. From that vantage point, he did look like some sort of language god, larger than life. My last living mentor, save for Panchal.

"*Ciao*, Ramona. *A che cosa devo l'onore?*"

Doc was fluent in eleven languages and conversational in twenty-two—something that made nice cocktail conversation, but that wasn't nearly as impressive to most Americans as it was to me. It was a game we liked to play, one of us started speaking in one language and you answered in another, until finally Doc broke into Swahili or a dead language no one spoke anymore—something only word nerds like us would enjoy.

I presented him with the dissertation, fifty typed pages.

"*A língua do amor?*"

Portuguese. Nice move. I responded in German, "*Für dein Lesevergnügen.*"

He laughed, his white beard catching the lights of the stage. "My reading pleasure, eh? I'll be the judge of that."

Ten Children's Products I Refuse to Order Because They Sound Too Much Like BDSM Accessories and I Need to Keep My NSA Profile Low

1. Vinyl Punisher
2. Double pounding bench
3. Ring and trap combo
4. Deluxe Monkey Bouncer
5. Hammer Balls
6. Whipslammer
7. Elephant harness
8. Drop-seat pajamas
9. Glow-in-the-dark Gimp
10. Erector set

Book Club Cheat Sheet

First of all, congratulations for being in a book club. That is totally great. I was in a book club once, for about three months. I made it to two meetings, ate about eleven free bagels, and "read" one of the books—by which I mean I read the first chapter, skimmed the middle, and glanced at the ending. That, I have found, is usually enough to get by in a book club, especially if yours serves booze. I hope you arrived at this page because you actually read the whole book chronologically, stopping only to binge-watch your favorite TV show or make nachos, but just in case you weren't able to finish it in time, here are some things to say or ask that will make it sound like you read the whole book really closely:

- Is Una a reliable narrator? Would the book have been better told from the perspective of someone else, like Holden Caulfield, or Janice Dickinson?
- Una compares herself, physically, to men many times in the book. Is this just overcompensating for her rampant insecurity with aggressive self-deprecation, or does she suffer from traditional Freudian penis envy?
- Based on the rampant lies she admits to in "Late

Bloomer," is it possible that "Jeff" does not exist? Assuming that's the case, who helps Una zip up her ill-fitting Anthropologie purchases?

- I felt the book was Kafkaesque in its surreal distortion, sense of impending danger, and copious references to *The Real Housewives* franchise.

- This book changed my life. After reading it, I deleted my online cart full of Old Navy formal gaucho overalls and filled a garbage can with expired Nair bottles, cheap liquor, and Adidas shower shoes, which I then set ablaze. Mistake. I had to call the fire department, but while they extinguished my lawn I had time to reflect on my residual feelings for Rider Strong from *Boy Meets World*. Then, once the firefighters left, I resisted the urge to text my friends with an invented sexual encounter, and instead binge-watched old *Friends* episodes while eating a replica of the Taj Mahal I had constructed out of Pringles and Marshmallow Fluff. I feel pretty much the same as if I had gone to an ashram or been struck by lightning. I'm a better person, a better friend, a better lover, *and* I'm more respectful of others when sharing a public restroom experience. How can I nominate this book for a Nobel Prize, preferably via text or e-mail?